EMPOWERED LIVING

EMPOWERED LIVING

A Guide to
Being Your True Self

Antoinette Levine

BALBOA.
PRESS

A DIVISION OF HAY HOUSE

Penelope Love – Editor
Carol Green – Copy writer – editor, Back cover copy
Juliana Sankaran-Felix, Graphic Designer – Seven Section's Title Quote Pages
Julia Lendl-Celotto – Author Photo
Oliver Sadowitz, Illustrator – Chakra Illustration

Balboa Press books may be ordered through booksellers or by contacting:

Balboa Press
A Division of Hay House
1663 Liberty Drive
Bloomington, IN 47403
www.balboapress.com
1-(877) 407-4847

ISBN: 978-1-4525-4667-4 (sc)
ISBN: 978-1-4525-4668-1 (hc)
ISBN: 978-1-4525-4666-7 (e)

Library of Congress Control Number: 2012901829

Because of the dynamic nature of the Internet, any web addresses or links contained in this book may have changed since publication and may no longer be valid. The views expressed in this work are solely those of the author and do not necessarily reflect the views of the publisher, and the publisher hereby disclaims any responsibility for them.

The author of this book does not dispense medical advice or prescribe the use of any technique as a form of treatment for physical, emotional, or medical problems without the advice of a physician, either directly or indirectly. The intent of the author is only to offer information of a general nature to help you in your quest for emotional and spiritual well-being. In the event you use any of the information in this book for yourself, which is your constitutional right, the author and the publisher assume no responsibility for your actions.

Any people depicted in stock imagery provided by Shutterstock are models, and such images are being used for illustrative purposes only. Certain stock imagery ©Shutterstock.

Print information available on the last page.

Balboa Press rev. date: 10/03/2016

In Loving Memory of my Dad and brother Phillip

"Advice is like snow;
the softer it falls,
the longer it dwells upon,
and the deeper it sinks
into the mind."
~Mahatma Gandhi

CONTENTS

THE SEVEN SACRED CENTERS

I ~ UNITY

II ~ INTEND CREATE

III ~ INTEGRITY IN-TU-ITE

IV ~ HEART POWER

V ~ YIELD TO...WHAT IS...

VI ~ TRUTH FLOW...

VII ~ ONE PRESENCE

ACKNOWLEDGEMENTS

To my birth family, extended family of friends, the traditional and integrative practitioners named within these pages: I send you eternal appreciation, gratitude of the highest order. For I am here now thriving in the love you have shown. And that you continue to shower on my blessed Life.

Penelope Love, editor divine whose patient presence guided me through uncharted waters, I bow to your greatness. Thank you for believing in my spirited vision.

A few loving souls not named within these pages, though radiantly present while this book unfolded I thank you with all my heart: Maribel and Cecilio Gordillio, Lorenzo Casco, The Coaches Training Institute colleagues, The Shift Network's Soulful Women's Mythic Life Course members. With particular thanks to: Ashae, Deborah, ElizaBeth, Mary, Kalibri and Tasha.

And to a lifetime of visible and Invisible Teachers, and countless mentors who supported my evolving being. You are forever appreciated for your gracious guidance and encouragement to be my truest Self.

AN INVITATION

The age of enlightened consciousness calls us. There is a compelling immediacy to its wake up call. The time for exponential change— has arrived. Has your radiant Inner Being awakened? Quite likely, for you were drawn to this book, and are on the planet during this age of tremendous Awakening.

We are meant to be—a community of clear mindedness—amidst world-wide confusion. Here to reset the course of humankind by remembering Who We Are.

Eternal Source energy is the essence of all human Beings. We are Spirits in human form, walking on an evolutionary path with known or undiscovered gifts. A Universal invitation to walk a purposeful life beckons us with its call. We are inevitably called to find our way to a life that contributes to the Whole. Everyone has unique gifts to offer.

What is your vision of our future with Mother Earth? What were you born to share? A joyful clarity of direction awaits you when you remember what you came here for. Your open Heart will soar as it leads the way!

May your inborn gifts be reclaimed with grace and ease. This is my wish for all human Beings. I went kicking and screaming to reunite with my natural gifts. You don't have to go that way—unless you do.

Compassionate love resuscitated my life. It gives us this book. I share with you what I learned, so that we may ALL thrive and enjoy the abundance of Life.

Sadly, society perpetuates a politic of fear, greed and separation. It is a spiritually bankrupt system that mass-markets false happiness. We've been sold centuries of enduring lies that diminish and debilitate humanity. When we buy in to them, we remain trapped in a programmed mind-state. There's no joy, only worry, sorrow and suffering when one buys in to this societal conditioning.

True joy is simply in being Who We Really Are. Reconnecting with our Authentic Self, allows all that we need to arise from within. Eventually we witness our needs manifesting into form quite naturally. This experience is accessible to everyone through the *process* of conscious change.

The quality of our consciousness changes the quality of our lives. We don't control the process, only our commitment to cooperate and *be* with our inner work. Releasing conditioned-mind's resistance we uncover our best next steps. Source manages the rest.

If we are in despair or depression—suffering for any reason, whatever it is, it is a sacred invitation. *What is*—right here, right now—offers an entry way that leads to becoming spiritually empowered. *Now* is our moment-to-moment earthly classroom.

Our relationships, with people-places-things, mirror for us. Reflect for us what we are valuing, allow us to remember what we forgot. Once we accept our invitation to remember, the Invisible generously assists: Guides us onward. Commitment to consistent awareness reveals our True Heart's freedom.

My radical lessons led to a deep inner peace. Love's gentle strength eased a fear-based thinking that had blinded me from seeing, feeling my heart's unimaginable power. Fear still attempts to creep in. Thought forms of control and worry are witnessed with open-hearted Love. Spirit quiets falseness.

Freedom from fear—is our birthright.

How good it feels, once we have gone through what we must. Inner wisdom and freedom bloom as we *be with* life. Surrender—yielding to the flow of *what is*. Reunite with the ocean of peace that rests inside us. Peace is a powerful heart-centered feeling.

As we do our inner work, returning to Heart again and again. Uncaused joy awakens. It is our divine right to enjoy living. I staked my life on this Truth.

This book is an invitation for you—to return to your heart center—and enjoy embracing the raw, the passionate, the mysterious JOY of Life.

Awakening to Our True Power

Source called me back to Life and invited me to remember my eternal soul's divine destiny of wisdom walker. To be a way-shower, teach by example. Invitation accepted. I trust Universal Law, Source-God-All-That Is. I am grounded in a spiritual translation of our electromagnetic energy field's dynamic. I write this book from a spirit-mind-body perspective, Tao informed.

Visits with death, and a transformative healing, fused my thirty-one-year immersion in spiritual metaphysics, psychology, philosophy and the study of world religions—and awakened a calling to teach what I have *experientially* learned.

Tao means how: how things happen. *How things happen* is not the same as *what we should do*. No one can tell us what to do. This is our responsibility, our freedom.

We are eternal Source energy consciousness, within a unique transient human personality. Universal Energy moves through us. Our awareness of this enlivening connection—this Unity—is essential to understanding our innate ability to co-create.

Our conscious connection with Source is paramount to realizing co-creative change in our lives. **Embracing this essential Truth is our initial step toward Self-empowerment.**

Our personal spiritual power is Source energy, which flows, vibrates throughout our physical being. With our awareness, we *feel* its charge, its pulse. Our *feeling* sense ability is our primary tool towards *accessing* and *aligning* with conscious change.

Mindful breath is our key connective step. We accept breath upon arrival. We release our final breath when we depart. Breath is our absolute unity with, Who We Are—Love—Life itself.

None of us have to wait to accept our greatness, our true Nature. Most of us must let go of the disempowering-stories from our past. Detaching from any 'trauma-drama' so that our consciousness can expand. We are born great, and inner release work reconnects us with our intrinsic greatness.

As we raise our consciousness, we change our world. This requires our intentional attention: a commitment to practicing gentle witnessing of our thoughts/emotions/words/actions. We become present, surrendering the conditioned mind's habit of past-future fear-based thinking. We want to capably allow alignment with Source energy. All forms of resistance block this connection. Our transformation occurs in a state of *released resistance*.

First we must unlearn what we were taught about *how* things happen. The art of successful change requires we adhere to Universal Law: *inner cause creates outer effect*.

The quality of our thoughts generates a particular emotional frequency. Our emotional frequency signals our powerful Life Force energy— which in turn manifests an outcome. This is the nature of how we create our reality. Be it consciously or unconsciously by default. The spiritual science of universal creation just *is*. It is Universal Law. And it is ours to learn and enjoy creating with.

Talking about change is insufficient. Our conscious, proactive steps are essential. They open us to receive the abundant goodness

Universal Law will provide in our lives. We are infinitely loved. Well-being IS our fundamental state. Breath to breath, I learned that *we need to relax and breathe*—to *be* with the *experience* of life. **Once I unified—with Invisible Source, my body and life circumstances healed and thrived.**

Source's knowing of our true Nature is infinitely greater than our misinformed sense of self. We are Its beloved creations. When we awaken our Source-energy consciousness, we feel inspired to upgrade our thought-emotion transmissions. Choice, intention and inspired action become available. We begin to co-create, create our circumstances consciously.

Source energy is the power we came here to be one with. We want to experience the infinite possibilities of our earthly playground, enjoying one another and all we delight in.

This is heart-led living, to playfully co-create, having examined and shifted — the thought-emotion forms that once blocked our unity with Source.

It is also the way of living a wholly Unified Life.

Source Energy Bridge
•The Chakra System•

Learning to listen to Source energy's *spirit speak*, from head to toe, supports our change ability and connects us with our spirit-mind-body integration process. Its electromagnetic energy flows through every molecule within our human form, including our commonly referred to "personal space."

Three major channels (nadis) distribute life force energy, Kundalini ("serpent goddess") energy, which originates from the main river of our central channel's (sushumna) flow. It flows from the base of our spine through to the crown of our head. Snaking spirals of ascending and descending (ida and pingala nadis) energy currents further distributes vital energy through our entire organism. Our channels, rivers of energy, regulate seven vertically aligned centers—*the chakras*. This book teaches how to utilize our human energetic system---specifically, the chakra system's seven Life Processes, which can also be thought of as States of Consciousness Expansion---as a proactive pathway toward change.

The chakras, often called "wheels" or disks, are organizational centers that receive, assimilate and express life force energy. Sacred Eastern science defined them as source centers of transformation and healing—a seven-level philosophical model of the universe. This ancient science parallels modern archetypes of an individual's seven distinct interfacing stages of spiritual maturation and personal evolution.

Each chakra's Life Process represents specific spiritual lessons and common life challenges relative to that energy center. This book guides you through the interrelated and evolving Life Processes intrinsic to each Chakra Stage.

Knowledge of our chakra system was paramount to my integrative and overall recovery. As a supplemental practice, Kundalini yoga assisted (and still assists) me in opening and balancing Source energy flow. It became a key component in my spirit-mind-body integrative-healing process once I was healthy enough to engage in its fiery intensity with an expert teacher. As well as learning to modify according to my entire being's needs.

This practice was specifically helpful in my case, because kundalini energy rises through our central nervous system and manages our entire bio-energy system. Unified with our breath ("prana" vital energy) when chakra energy flows freely, we gain access to spiritual maturity and physical well-being.

The divine energy that courses through our bodies gives us our power. The Kundalini energy that winds around our spine, from its base in the first chakra to the crown of our heads, spirally transports the two contrasting energies of our psyche and physical body. The chakra "stages" represent seven interactive levels of our spiritual biology. Each stage contains a higher truth of our spiritual power. We are personally empowered by right use of each chakra's truth.

We are born with these truths interlaced throughout our biological energy system. They came in with us at birth, from the

Universal Energy we came from. The chakra system speaks of the human body's interconnectivity with Source energy.

Our ability to manage our personal power increases in tandem with a gradual intensification of Source energy flowing through us. When we allow this energy to flow unhindered throughout our body. Our spiritual expansion process is experienced as an invigorating, grounded allowance of this life-transforming energy.

The upward direction of our central channels' energy distribution through our chakra centers matters: from the ground up. This is representative of humanity's reliance on Earth energy, the sustaining ground for embodying ethereal consciousness. As such, the state of our individual chakra system is integral to our overall openness and connection with humankind's Highest Goodness.

Our lower-chakra development supports our higher energy centers' inspired guidance. All chakras contain unique **Life Processes** that present specific human-developmental challenges and maturing spiritual qualities—of daily life. As we practice and gain mastery of our thought-emotion choices, we access the energy empowerment of each chakra—and in this teaching each chakra is referred to as one of **Seven Stages**. The chakra stages represent and reveal where our life force is currently in or out of balance. Through introspection we soon realize that every choice we make, in relation to any stage, reflects *Pure Love* or *base fear*.

Our quest is to nurture energetic wholeness, allow full openness. If these pages are viewed as a field of fertile seeds, and awareness as vital nourishment—then full bloom Wholeness is our destiny as we focus our attention and allow an integration of the spirit-mind-body power of all Seven Stages.

Understanding each stage's significance lends clarity to where we currently are on our path. It gives us a reference point along our way. We gain an ability to notice the unique spiraling of our mind-emotion process. We become Self-empowered to notice when, where, and how we stagnate, block or open our vital life force. With increased evidence of the power that unobstructed energy provides, we observe inner-outer shifts representative of alignment with Source energy flow.

As you explore Stages One through Seven, your understanding of the chakras, and how you choose to utilize this book, will gently unfold. The universally acknowledged bio-physical location of each chakra is described at the opening of each **Life Process** description (to familiarize yourself with each chakra's general location at a glance, please reference the **Illustration of Chakra System**) Though their specific locales may vary slightly from person to person, their overall relationship to one another is consistent.

Drawing from this biological wisdom-map, I offer both knowledge and my direct experience of our mind-emotion development as we interact with and consciously embody, make tangible and effective, the wisdom of the Seven Stages.

The potent stories from my near-death-to-joyful healing serve as an example of one person's unique road map (hazardous detours included). Allow the **Passages** of my personal story to inspire reflections on your journey while utilizing the **Self-Inquiry** exercises which complete each stage's module.

I recommend settling into a relaxed state and connecting with your Highest Self when embarking upon introspective questions. You may notice that my physical dilemmas manifested in chakra centers representative of resistance to Source energy flow. Your conscious awareness of the blockages created by my decisions and behaviors may assist in clearing similar energies in your field.

These are my experiences only and if you sense any emotional memory or reactivation trigger, please give yourself time to stop and breathe deeply, listening to what your Heart reveals to you. Allow yourself to **go gently. . .**

Overview of the Seven Stages:
What They Symbolize

This overview of our chakra system summarizes the spiritual life-lessons the **Seven Stages** represent. Full descriptions are further articulated in each section of the book. Our charkas' spiraling pathway's ascending (spirit-mind) energy currents and descending (soul-body) currents'—free flow, stagnant or blocked—nature reflect the overall well being of our chakras' integrated state.

Our chakra centers are most likely, by adulthood, interactively in development with variances in degrees of functionality. Openness and balance develops further as we consciously free ourselves from the conditioning of familial and societal imprints. A committed spiritual seeker's basic instinctual reactivity is gradually transmuted into a conscious response to life. Allowance of wisdom and understanding, while grounded in our physical body, lights our path to Wholeness and Freedom. Our journey begins from the ground up!

Stage One (first 'root' chakra) lessons arise from family-of-origin as well as group environments and challenges pertaining to our grounded stability in the material world. As we individuate, head out into the world and interact with others, **Stage Two** (second

9

chakra) lessons encompass our partnerships, relationships, and power of choice. Energy at this stage reflects how we manage our attitudes about sex, money and outer relations, relative to our physical desires. As we mature **Stage Three** (third chakra) energy symbolizes our evolving sense of self. Center three holds the energy of our maturing ego personality, self-worth and self-esteem. As we move into **Stage Four** (heart chakra), our center of emotional power contains lessons related to love, forgiveness and compassion. Here we meet our core power, fueled by our biological and spiritual heart. Our key wheel of energy, its openness empowers lower and upper energy centers. Our heart center is Essential Energy which fuels our entire integrative direction and completeness. Its energy assists us with realignment of lower-chakra energetic imbalances, while equally empowering us to integrate upper energy centers. **Stage Five** (fifth chakra) energy lessons relate to our use of will and self-expression in unison with the energy fueling our power of choice. This stage's openness offers us an ability to receive inspiration infused by six and seventh energy centers and act upon expression of them, particularly when created in unison with lower center's worldly and grounded strengths.

Stage Six (sixth chakra) center's "third eye" is representative of our evolving ability to receive insight, wisdom and higher levels of the intuitive mind. **Stage Seven** (seventh chakra) our "crown chakra" aligns us with lessons related to spirituality, the transcendent dimensions of life. It is our connection to Higher Consciousness.

The associated lessons of each stage, when met with our conscious practices, grow our confidence. As we mature spiritually, our personal power and self-knowledge integrate with spirit. Our alignment with Source energy is a dynamically evolving process of progression. Often the next stage must begin before the stage below opens fully.

We continue to revisit stages throughout our lives. Our outer life choices are upgraded as our consciousness expands and chakras open more fully.

To Recover...Our Self

My overall recovery process increased my recognition of "recovery movements" in general. We all want to recover our true Self. Respecting our body's eco-system is critical to this process. Honoring the health of our respiratory and spinal functionality is primary. The allowance of universal energy flow is essential to honoring our well-being.

Movement and conscious breath work are advocated throughout the elements of this book. Our spinal health is of significant importance in this context. Thus it is suggested to choose a movement and practice with appropriate measure: Hatha and or Kundalini yoga, tai chi, martial arts or simple stretch exercises, coupled with regular cardio care support and strengthen our mind-body connection. Through utilizing any of these practices (and others), we explore and discover our best, focused-breath practices. Conscious breathing is a go-to fundamental of living an aware life. Every-day task can be utilized with conscious awareness as well.

The regular practice of stillness in a meditative state with the spine erect, in a distraction-free environment, is essential to begin witnessing and quieting the mind. This ergonomic position facilitates conscious breathing, as we gain access to inner calm and a capacity for improved awareness in our daily lives.

About Book Design + Spiral Process Progress

Personal shifts inspire (and often are inspired by) new ways of experiencing familiar things. Rather than traditional "chapters" I offer a unique unfolding in ascending order of the Seven Stages. Interwoven within each Stage is my story's **Passages**—of how I traversed fear-based thinking in to living from Love. These Passages are therapeutic storytelling/telling story intended to offer transformation and growth to everyone – reader and teller alike. Interspersed along the way, **Inspiration** vignettes role-model practices and share wisdom I gained and incorporated into my renewed way of life.

I have often learned how to do something by watching how not to do something. Equally, I've been inspired by watching someone's unique recovery-forward movement process. And so, telling my story offers what I learned through the process of reconnection-realignment with Source, allowing It as my sole guide. The journey from the less-than-best early stages of my story into transcendent experiences is intended to inspire your unique greatness.

Following each Stage's telling story, we will explore its chakra's **Life Process** in depth. This concentrated information is not designed to be absorbed or fully grasped in one sitting Akin to contemplative traditions, Life Process descriptions are yours to return to as often as you choose.

At the end of each stage, enjoy some deep breaths and partake in self exploration. The **Self-Inquiry** questions are there for you, to be visited and revisited whenever you feel called to delve into your inner work. Honoring ones transformative journey with contemplative inquiry remains a powerfully revealing practice for me.

A necessary element of transformation and change is to begin taking steps in our chosen direction. **Micro Moves** is an additional tool provided for anytime use. Given once in the back of the book, I invite you go there with open Hearted listening.

You may discover you have integrated certain stages or another, and want to utilize story, inspiration, information and self-inquiry simply as review prompts. Maybe you are a proficient co-creator with Source who wants to revisit earlier-stage's energy shifts while your Stage Six visionary qualities heighten. Or you know yourself as grounded and present in your energy field delighted to refresh your wisdom, utilizing all elements of this book.

Spiral *Process*

We revisit many of the seven stage's lessons throughout our lives as we move in to consistent alignment with Source. Imagine *spirit-mind-body integration* being an ever-expanding spiral. As we respect process and patiently honor the potential for revisiting life lessons, our experience of life shifts—from the inside out. We grow to more fully enjoy life's mysterious adventures.

I invite you, sisters and brothers, to set your own gentle pace, stage-by-stage while being with this book. You may want to allow space and time to absorb the information of each stage before moving on to the next. Allowing yourself to experience and explore what comes up for you, from the depths of your Infinite being.

Please bring your Highest Self with you and decide what is true and resonant for you at this moment in your life. There is open space after each self-inquiry question for your notes. A handy journal is recommended to support your ongoing Inquiry notations. You know what is best!

Author's Introduction

Thank you for reading this opening story. It describes how I came to write this book.

A few years before transformative events, I printed, "Almighty Loving Creator, help me take a fresh look at everything" on a legal-sized sheet of paper. Writing in large capitals, I had connected the two 'o's' in 'look' with fat black dots. Cross-eyed silliness lightened up my seriously meant request to Source. I signed my name below an all-caps "Thank You!" Then I taped it to my inspiration wall. Signed sealed and delivered.

Request granted.

Comatose for two months, I awakened a middle-aged toddler. All knowledge and know-how had been lost. *What's my name? Where am I?* Multiple strokes and systemic lupus were a violent combination. I accept full responsibility. No one, no gene, no-thing outside myself bottomed me out. Dysfunctional ego dictates had run my life—away from the purposes of my soul. For decades ego-mind battled with my true heart's destiny.

God helped me hit rock bottom, picked me up inviting me to return and remember how to live life fully. My first heartfelt vision is to share my story and what I learned: a pathway to be with *what is*—as an integrative process to Wholeness.

Please join with me where this book's story Passages originated:

It was late spring 1956. Mom remembers our first face-to-face. The Queen of Angels Hospital nurse brought me in. "You had a very serious look on your little red face, no smile or expression like the first two."

In fetus, I had sensed not wanting to be a burden. A decision was made to be self-reliant.

Mom, now in her 80s, continued our long-distance phone chat. "When you were conceived, Michael was just nine months old. I didn't want to be pregnant again, not so soon." The rhythm method of birth-control, adopted by many 1950s Catholics contributed to a baby boom. Birth control was forbidden. My folks were devout.

Third in a row, I grew up an adult-child. Nicknamed "Granny" by the time I was three, I felt the weight of humanity pressed on my soft-skinned shoulders. Harboring a Joan of Arc archetype complex, I'd thought it was my duty to help save the world. I imagined being in the French

Resistance, while reading 'The Diary of Anne Frank", as my adventuress inner heroine gestated. Later on, I visualized myself supporting my favorite television heroes. Spock and Captain Kirk assigned me to intergalactic missions aboard the USS Enterprise.

The Pasadena, California, LeVine tribe grew to nine: six children with well-above-average IQs, and a younger brother born mentally impaired. Phillip's hydrocephalic challenges gave us an early initiation to being inclusively compassionate. Our multiracial,

Jewish-surnamed Catholic family turned heads. At state and national park campgrounds, we often drew curious stares. Well into the 1960s, interracial marriage, not legalized in some Southern states until 1967's Supreme Court decision, was most certainly not the norm.

My family-of-origin had a quirky sense of humor regarding societal distain. Dad declared us bull's-eye targets for Klu Klux Klan atrocities. A young sponge, I absorbed bread-winning DeWitt LeVine's gentle aerospace-engineer perfectionism and housewife-mother, Yvonne's loving ways of control. Young and smart they married against all odds in 1953 making a radical commitment to their seven children: "the kids come first, no matter what." Strident efforts to raise us to be productive citizens were administered. Education, religion, sports and great appreciation for Nature ruled the roost.

By age six, my little wise self had inwardly declared, *Be patient with mom and dad. They're young, they've got their hands full and are doing the best they can—don't make trouble.* I didn't. I went hard on myself instead. Unconscious of being extremely self-critical.

An unrecognized inner mantra as a little girl—faster, better, best—was my thematic self-imposed curriculum. I ignored early signs of artistic and intuitive gifts. Dad was startled when I brought him his Kodak camera, noting, "I was just going to get that." When Mom's mother died, I knew it. Auntie Gertrude had left a message for Mom to call. Before she returned the call, I said simply, "Grandma died."

Many youngsters display intuitive behaviors. I barely recognized them, choosing instead to fit in. I moved fast in that direction. Dutiful daughter tasks were executed with thoroughness, obedience and speed. I became a childhood perfectionist, a budding control addict. I doted, bossy at times, over younger siblings. I did not rebel.

Thank goodness for a world religions class at a Catholic all-girls high school. It opened my 'waiting for truth' mind. Eastern philosophy resonated strongly. Taoism felt truer than Catholic dogma. Books on spiritual metaphysics and self-realization joined my reading materials.

Drawn by a vision of the 'great escape' from familial restrictions, I plotted a route toward university. Efforts industriously began at age fifteen. They rewarded me with full-paid scholarship and admission to the University of California, Santa Barbara. I majored in psychology, began para-professional counseling and worked off campus as well. I was naively determined to trade my first authority figures for those that followed.

After a few years at U.C.S.B., ambition grew and I returned to Southern California. I was accepted as a U.C.S.B. Dean's List transfer student by University of Southern California's School of Journalism. I easily segued into being a paid student-athlete-peer counselor and teacher's assistant facilitator for undergraduate human development classes. In addition to working off campus at a Beverly Hills department store, I was also hired as a request operator at KHJ, a local LA radio station.

And so I jumped feet-first into the boiling kettle of a superficially successful life. Friends, family and colleagues may disagree. They were proud of me. On paper I was an achiever. I acknowledge that I consistently inspired and encouraged those around me, even while running after worldly gains. Inspirational leadership came naturally, though I underrated my creative abilities.

My non-stop employment history had begun, by choice, at age fourteen. I had wanted economic independence from my folks.

A U.S.C. graduation led to a thirty-year career in the Media and Motion Picture industries. World travel, property ownership in the U.S. and Mexico, appeared to be success from a worldly perspective. I felt off-balance—often.

Seeking outer solutions for inner dissonance became deadly. Thirty six years of striving for monetary increases and recognition was emotional poison. A colleague in the film industry referred to our careers as, "golden handcuffs." I wore mine willingly—falsely believing that I needed to prove my worth. I finally dropped—nearly dead, passed out on my bathroom floor. Chasing rewards for being worthy ended my delusion of unworthiness.

My handwritten request to Source had been answered. The reply took me down and returned me to life. Helped me "take a new look at everything." Co-operation was up to me. And all that was necessary. **Here we are. Let's go on!**

UNITY

L

O

V

E

Is

The

A

N

S

W

E

False Expectations Appear Real

First Inspiration

Most of us are familiar with the following universal call for Invisible support, peace and courage. Here is how I understand its offering:

"God grant me the Serenity to accept the things I cannot change
—anything other than ourselves and our life circumstances—
the Courage to change the things I can
—ourselves and our life circumstances—
and the Wisdom to know the difference."

Initially, Stage One wisdom arises from our common sense. Mindful awareness practices strengthen our inner resolve and invite higher and deeper wisdom. Wisdom expands stage by stage with committed practices.

As we revisit stages throughout our life in "spiral progressions," increased wisdom inspires our choice making. This is the Grace of our integrative process. As we courageously co-operate with Source, our spirit-mind-body integrates toward wholeness. Our challenges loosen their restrictive hold. Spirit lightens our heavy heart.

Heart is at the root of Courage. The Latin word 'cor' translates to heart. The English word *core* originated from "cor." Our core authentic Self—Inner Being—energizes us with Pure Love. In contrast to emotion-base love, Pure Love just is---for no reason other than Love.

Pure Love is the antidote for fear. Our Inner Being encourages us to live from and as Love. Our capacity to love and be love grows as we do our inner work. We watch as our outer world begins to change for the better. This heartfelt courage is our first step into a new already existing, dimension of Life. Our relationship with Life has changed. Serenity or "peace of mind" becomes a distinct possibility.

Recovery issues were woven into my family history for three generations. I share with you a late October 2011 e-mail exchange with my younger brother. Joseph Gerard, a recovered homeless-alcoholic, now employed as a Washington State-certified Peer Counselor who advocates for others. He deeply inspired my recovery journey as well. May our heartfelt words give you unbendable courage, and inspire your self-exploration and daily Life. Welcome!

Antoinette,

Sometimes what you say is beyond me, but I understood this. *Although the arrival of the Aquarian Age and shifts on the planet are exciting developments,* it is a little scary to me. I feel that I will need to expect more from myself and I hope I am up to the challenge. :)

Love & Bright Blessings,
Joseph

★ ★ ★

Joseph,

Yes, more is needed from us all...but we must go inside and relate with our Inner Light (our individual soul energized by Universal spirit) for guidance. It is simply easier and wisest—and truly the only way to go through what we must go through. What is now and forever changing around us will change for the highest good, if we participate with Heart.

Please do ask yourself, *"What is my best spiritual support system, structure and reliable resource at this time in my life?"* Lean into it—whatever it is. Trust your inner "old" wise Self's whispers, voice and intuition. It offers deeper wisdom than common sense and intellect combined.

All-Ways feel free to speak your truth with loving kindness, no matter what those around you believe.

It is an Inside job. It is what recovery is All about. Recovering our trust in our inner Self, we breathe and go, one foot, one step, one day at a time.

I hope this enhances your daily living possibilities as you expand with continued growth. The Real you inside is up for anything. The power of the Universe is inside us all—God, Source. Part of the lie earthly Beings are sold is that we have to buy-pay a church or other outer entity for our well-being and daily prosperity.

Humor is good, a form of play with Source energy to lighten the darkness.

Another helpful daily bread is Abraham-Hick's Publications e-mail offerings: dailyquote@abraham-hicks.com

Love and blessings beyond time and space...
xoAntoinette

Fight and Flight

It startled me. In an instant, I'd forgotten how to drive. Where do my feet go? I clinched the steering wheel. It was the only thing to hold onto.

I had needed gasoline. The Shell station across from Burbank's NBC "Tonight Show" studios was ahead on the right. I turned into its Alameda Avenue driveway. My midnight-blue Tahoe lurched, bounced and rocked up over the curb. Driving was a necessary part of my profession in the film industry: Location Management. I ignored this hiccup. Pushing past a telling moment, I drove toward the pumps—ignorant of the danger I brought to myself and everyone in the vicinity.

Suddenly, slow motion surrounded me. The brake pedal wasn't where my brain had told my foot to go. Every element of driving had become muddled. It was a minor stroke.

A parked taxi driver had witnessed this odd driving demonstration. A uniformed attendant rapidly exited the station's mini-market. He offered to pump the gas. I was shaken and confused. I knew how to drive. What had happened?

Neither gentleman thought I would be safe to drive home. I agreed. Thank goodness, no one was harmed. Front bumper damage was noted. One of the men parked the slightly dented Tahoe out on Olive Avenue for me. After driving me home safely, the taxi driver gave me his card. Offering future help if needed. I lost memory of what occurred next.

★   ★   ★

After all that followed, those split-second memories would eventually resurface. No matter the brain and bodily damage yet to unfold, this vivid recollection waited in cerebral safekeeping. Now, I am able to open this story from its beginning.

There'd been other warning signs before the loss of cognition at the fuel pumps. Suspected arthritis had been ailing me for several months. Joint stiffness and an achy muscle history started in December 2006. I had noted a history of experiences and saved them in my computer. This condition began while on hiatus between film production projects. I was living at my little condo on the Mayan Riviera. My friends in the Yucatan Peninsula were concerned. I was a healthy traveler and an avid scuba diver. My lethargy was highly irregular.

Lavonna Redman, founder of Angel Notion, a non-profit community health center in Playa del Carmen, took me to one of her trusted doctors. Multiple joint aches continued. A cold graduated to a relentless low-grade flu. As a constant fatigue settled in, I carried on. I wouldn't stop. I iced my knees as the pain became increasingly uncomfortable. I was unable to sleep.

I traveled back to Los Angeles unconvinced I needed professional medical attention. I was stubborn and ignored growing evidence of a critical health condition. The pain waned in and out. I coped.

A consummate work-a-holic I sought my next fix. It was to be a February 2007 Disney CBS pilot. I kept up my supervising location-manger high-pressured pace the best I could. As one of a film crew's collective department heads, I took my work seriously. I acted like I was fine in meetings and presentations with the director and producers. I was tired all the time.

While out finding and negotiating suitable locations, I had to pull over and nap. Thankfully I had hired Nathan Stein to once again be my key assistant. We had become a dynamic duo in my twenty-three years of staffing location departments.

Nathan recalls our *Carpooler's* pilot prep and film days: *"Antoinette, we were all worried about you. We knew something was seriously amiss. You'd never ever been sluggish or tired before. You were always the epitome of high energy. It was weird. You were very slow and deliberate with walking. Your attitude was that you were seeking treatment in your own way. People thought you should be seeing a doctor or primary care."*

I remember needing to go sleep in my car after the day's filming began. Once my early-morning-shoot day duties were complete, Nate would take over for me. My visits to a naturopath and acupuncturist raised my expectations. I wanted to figure out what was wrong. Why wasn't I getting any better? The naturopath decided we needed blood tests.

We had been experimenting with non-conclusive allergy testing. Then he called. It must have been soon after the Shell station display of reckless driving.

"Antoinette, there's something off with your blood tests. Go to your nearest emergency room immediately. Don not drive," he warned.

I felt panicky, my heart raced. A cab driver dropped me at Providence St. Joseph's Medical Center Emergency Room entrance. Hospital admission forms were filled out with shaky clammy hands. My knees buckled as I leaned into the ER counter and waited for a room. I felt short of breath from fear. Friends recall being called or text messaged while I waited. I don't remember how this happened.

Body Smarts

Nate received a call I was at St. Joseph's emergency room. News spread between a few of my closest friends. Ardice Faoro, Carmen Thomas-Paris, Jessica Estrada-Petterson, Cathy Carr, Donna Schwartz-Mills and Wendy Ferren-Van Syckle were all informed. They are friends you'll hear from as this story unfolds. I might have called Regina Rose, my younger sister and friend, but don't remember how my family was informed. Nathan or the hospital might have called. My hospital admission stunned everyone. I had kept my downward health condition completely under wraps, not wanting to hurt my reputation in the film business. It was one of my deepest fears. We were only as good as the work we can perform. And I was in bad shape. My family hadn't been told about my abnormal health condition either.

Nathan hurried to the hospital. He found me lying on an ER gurney. I remember the moisture in his eyes as he watched. His mentor and friend—flattened out—shivering and burning up with fever. Nathan's recollection of that first admission: *"It made me sad and scared, not knowing what was going on, but also relieved that traditional care was being provided."*

With a previous history of solid health, I never had a primary care provider. Motion Picture Insurance is phenomenal—I could have gone to the Toluca Lake Health Center the minute I returned from Mexico. I never considered it an option. I had always looked to alternative medicine for my health care needs. I also dismissed traditional medicine as a solution to what ails us. Firmly ensconced in my beliefs, common sense had been absent.

I was fortunate that March 2007 evening. Dr. Stephen M. Taback was called in. A St. Joseph's Medical Center cardio-pulmonary physician with a private practice as well, he would become my extraordinary primary physician by default. When I researched how he came to be my physician, I found irony in his reply, *"I see all the admitted Motion Picture patients that come into the hospital."* He is on the MPI physicians list I had failed to investigate.

In the swirl of the evening, my former blood tests were obtained. More were taken. The stroke event wasn't yet in the mix. Family caught planes, friends drove over. This was an unusual occurrence.

Cathy decorated the wall beside my hospital bed with shiny tropical fish cutouts. Everyone knew how much I loved communing with our underwater world's beauty and uniqueness. Carmen's gift: a string of colorful lights accented Jessica's photo collage of friend's gatherings and celebrations. They wanted to cheer me up and also give evidence to nurses and doctors of who I am in their lives. Orderlies would eventually assist in bringing the photo collage along as I traveled the hospital room to room.

Regina, my sister/friend arrived from Seattle and stayed in my nearby condo. I answered her question: *"What happened to your car? It has a dent on the front end…"* with a *"No, it doesn't."* I was experiencing short-term memory loss with no recollection of the brain seizure.

I was also distraught at missing my godson Marco Petterson's baptism. Jessica, a longtime friend, former location assistant (now my "co-madre"), had chosen me to be a spiritual presence in Marco's life. Her husband Robert and she were only concerned with my getting better.

Wendy, a friend and former '80s radio-days colleague, now a studio executive, brought me light-hearted movies from Paramount Picture's collection. It's what I asked for, to watch once I returned home. We were all relatively hopeful at this point. Our radio-programming research colleague Donna Schwartz-Mills wrote in her blog, *"Her health problems gave me a shock. As long as I have known her she's done everything right. She was on her university track team and always had a daily workout regime. She watches what she eats and tries to live her life in balance."* Donna's blog notes reflect the hospital's comment regarding my health history: **unremarkable.**

But my history was changing by the hour. Dr. Taback requested a rheumatology consultation. Dr. Wonil Lee, a highly regarded private practice rheumatologist, confirmed Dr. Taback's suspicions. Systemic lupus had been added to my once unremarkable medical history.

CVA (cerebral vascular accident) history waited in the wings, unbeknownst to my physicians, who were focusing on vital-sign stabilization. I was placed on high doses of steroids and numerous other pharmaceuticals to address fever and infections. Even though my condition wasn't extreme for a hospital staff, it was the shock of my life—up to that point.

More shocking than the hospitalization was being involuntarily stopped. For the first in thirty-six years, I was told *not to work.*

This required a greater adjustment than a dis-ease diagnosis. Ardice and Carmen heard me say that I wanted to get better and start looking for my next project. Source had other plans.

Based on Elizabeth Kubler-Ross' stages of grief, I was in a first-stage state of denial. The tide had been turned *for* me—yet I was completely unaware that this outer event was a precursor of a tumultuous, yet often sought after, major inner shift.

Home Alone

Now I was released from a "first time in my life" hospitalization. The initial March 2007 stroke event had gone undetected. The doctor's main focus was on my highly imbalanced blood-test results. It would be several years before I regained my brain's initial stroke memory shared in 'Fight or Flight'. Medical discharge records from the seven-day admission confirmed: acute systemic lupus. Secondary to lupus, a brain seizure threat silently loomed.

The clinical social worker's discharge notes stated that I understood the newly diagnosed condition and was anxious—an admitted "control issues" personality type.

In truth, I was in a state of shock, leaving the hospital stunned by an unexpected medical condition. Unable to return to work, I had no idea what lupus was. The predisposition for stroke and lupus in my ambitious lifestyle was stress. And I recognized that I had been over-thinking, overworking and stressing my body since childhood. I'd become identified with, attached to---having a clean bill of health. I covered up a resistant disposition with denial and delusional hopefulness.

Though I had reviewed Louise L. Hay's *You Can Heal Your Life*, I didn't adhere to its metaphysical teachings. Spiritual metaphysics would eventually be a consciously revisited component of my recovery process. Louise Hay's recommended affirmations regarding lupus rang an unheeded bell. It spoke to alignment with authentic self-love. I hadn't looked at the cerebral vascular accident (stroke) affirmations until much later: *"Life is change. I adapt easily to new. I accept life. Past present and future."*

I was so out of control, grasping at holding onto control, Inner or outer sage advice could not be heard. In-home daytime nursing care had been hired. They were discontinued after the first few weeks. Nate, Cathy and other friends visited when they could. I vaguely remember Cathy helping me figure out how to use my computer. Attend to online banking and other internet chores. I wasn't used to asking for help, though now I needed assistance to handle ordinary tasks.

My tough-as-nails, "I can handle it" attitude eventually resurfaced. I expected an instantaneous solution. The medication's side effects were extremely disorienting, physically and psychologically. My heretofore healthy track record seldom required medicinal supplements. The most I would ingest by choice were homeopathic aids for colds or sore throat. While I lived in a medicated fog of despair, my life circumstances had changed with frightful abruptness. High doses of steroids and additional medications added to my unfocused state of mind. I was unconsciously grieving a much coveted "bill of great health." For a former university-level competitive athlete and world-traveled scuba diver, this was not the life I'd become accustomed to. I wanted my old life back, right now! I was impatient and ornery.

Nathan recalls my expectations about work: *"You were thinking we might go on the series of the pilot we had just shot."* But Nate saw a glimmer of hope in that cloud of delusion. Maybe I was getting a clue when "Desperate Housewives" Supervising Location Manager, David Foster called. He wanted my assessment of Nathan as a key assistant. *"'I don't know when I'm going to start my next project—so if Nathan Stein is on the availability list, you'd be doing yourself a big favor to hire him immediately."* David did. Nate, normally the first on my team to be hired, had secured work for years to come. I was relieved. That's as close as I came to surrender.

A 2011 review of my journal scribbles dated late May 2007 revealed that something had gone terribly wrong. My handwriting resembled that of a young child. A check I had attempted to write was illegible. Misshapen letters and numbers scrawled evidence of my brain's imbalanced state. No one knew of my condition. I was proud and stubborn, even while I spiraled toward collapse.

Rheumatologist Dr. Wonil Lee's hospital records are telling: *"She was diagnosed with systemic lupus. We treated with 60mg of prednisone per day. Over the next two months, her condition showed signs of improvement. She developed a mild case of steroid-induced psychosis. She had difficulty sleeping with cognitive dysfunction and we lowered to dose to 10mg per day and added 200mg of Plaquenil. She was found to have an Escherichia coli urinary tract infection and prescribed Kelflex. However repeat culture showed same infection and she received Levaquin before Memorial Day weekend. I spoke with the patient 2-3 days before that weekend and she said she felt fine."*

My Joan of Ark heroine act did not pay off.

I was nervous and jittery, feeling out of my mind. Nate remembers visiting. He put me on the phone with his dad, a certified registered nurse anesthetist. I also spoke with my brother-in-law, John Bothell, in a similar profession. *"Be careful with those medications. Follow the doctor's instructions,"* they warned. I accepted their advice, yet gradually became erratic and disoriented, forgetful if or when I'd taken the multiple medications. I had lost short-term memory. I began trying to keep notes—writing myself writing myself reminders of what I had done. Stumbling through time, I was a home-alone 50-year-old in a drama of own her making.

First Flirt

By June 1st, my 51st birthday had come and gone. I was unusually absent. Birthday celebrations, to one degree or another, were a personal tradition. Family and friends hadn't heard from me for nearly a week. Not responding to e-mails or phone messages was highly irregular, especially after my emergency hospitalization.

Regina activated a recently collected e-mail tree, contacting my LA-area friends. Carmen, Ardice, Cathy and others exchanged correspondence leaving voice messages to no avail. Nate was on a road trip to Washington D.C. to visit his girlfriend, Lisa. Los Angeles is vast geographically and my friends do not live near-by. Electronic communication had become a routine means of contact. My next-door neighbors were not aware of my debilitated condition. I had pride-fully kept it to myself.

Mom, homebound in Seattle's outer suburbs, demanded: "Find Antoinette!" Regina called the Burbank Police Department from Washington State. Their June 4th entry through an unlocked front door found me lying in my own bodily refuse, barely alive.

Paramedic reports described me as being in an altered mental state. Subsequent MRIs showed frontal and middle bi-lateral stroke events. There were also head-to-toe pressure wounds (decubitus ulcers) that were deep. My prone body's weight had blocked circulation for 5-7 days (no accurate record). 152 pounds of negative pressure had worn down and through the skin of my scalp, shoulder blades, heels and tailbone. The tailbone coccyx area ulcer was a wide cavernous sore. This massive stage IV sacral wound had penetrated through bone.

My brain and body had been severely damaged by a resistant ego-mind. I recognize this June 2007 moment as the first of several, when choice showed itself. Did I want to live or did I want to depart? Something in me chose to stick around, while I lay in my own urine and feces. I have no conscious memories of those "life in the balance" bathroom days.

When the Burbank Paramedic team removed my inert body, layers of dead skin peeled away. The hospital-record wound photos show where skin had peeled off my legs and buttocks during that urgent rescue.

Not until I researched the writing of this book did I realize why my older brother, Michael, retiled the faux marble bathroom floor. He had compassionately removed visual evidence of my first flirt with disintegration.

The ambulance ride delivered me to a hospital other than St. Joseph's. They had no knowledge or records of my eight-week-old medical history. I was evaluated by their cardiology, neurology, rheumatology and internal medicine physicians.

Carmen and Ardice were called in the early morning hours by Regina in Washington State. "Would you go to Antoinette at this hospital until Michael can arrive from San Diego?" They went. Found me a mess. Hair matted with my own excrement. I was spinal tapped, as were my friends, for meningitis.

The staff appeared to be without a clue. A heaven-sent nurse whispered to my friends as she walked passed, "Get her back to St. Joseph's." Michael heard my friend's adamant request. And saw the hospital's dark noisy environment. On June 8, 2007, I was readmitted to Providence St. Joseph's Medical Center, where lengthy lesson-filled days and nights lay ahead.

First Life Process

Our "root" chakra energy represents our family roots as well as our rootedness within extended "tribal" groups and our world communities. First chakra's tribal energy links us with our willpower, personal identity and belief patterns. It governs our survival instinct and energizes our ability to feel safe in life. Living capable of having what we need for protection and nourishment within our physical body and the body of our life circumstances. Developed and open, it reflects our healed and matured relationship choices within familial and societal systems and governmental law and order structures. The energetic state of our first chakra is reflective of our ability to not only maintain trust in the world, but also feel safe and deserving to receive what we need in order to provide for our basic human needs.

The first chakra is located at the base of our spine (specifically the coccyx) and represents our ability to be grounded in life. Our innate need for logic, structure and order is stabilized by its energy. Stability and security in our physical health, as well as the ability to provide for ourselves, mates and offspring with trust in life, are matured first chakra qualities. Its' thought-emotion challenges arise from a fear of survival or abandonment by a group, be it familial or societal in nature.

Symbolic of our reliance on Mother Earth's solid ground, first chakra energy's connection governs our body's feet, legs, spinal column, bones/bone marrow and our immune system. It represents our body-temple's energy framework and foundation with all of life. The organs governed include the rectum, large intestine, male reproductive organs and prostate. This potent container of grounding energy, the fuel of which nurtures our growth and exploratory journey of the upper six chakra centers, propels us beyond a mundane survival mentality and baseline existence.

Family and the First Chakra

Before we grow in conscious awareness, we first must meet the life challenges and lessons stemming from our original family environment. The first imprints of our mind-emotion faculties were etched into our body's energy field by the habits and behavior patterns learned since birth. These imprints create psychological factors that continue to color the way we lead our adult lives—until they are examined from a matured perceptive.

Our basic survival needs, all material matters of our first-chakra center, were initially met in relatively functional or dysfunctional manners. We were entirely reliant on parental figures, whether biological, adoptive, foster or institutional—for our basic needs: food, clothing, shelter, emotional support, safety and protection. If any or all of these elemental necessities were absent or distorted, we absorbed a psycho-emotional impact that has influenced our interpretation(s) of material reality.

Set in place anywhere from dysfunctional womb to birth and throughout our youth, childhood emotional imprints may present "root" energy stagnations or blocks well into our adulthood. Because they occurred so early in our lives, we are rarely conscious of them. Emotional issues with our biological or adoptive mother, when unresolved within our psychological makeup, stymie our grounded sense of self. Thus the root chakra is the center of nurturing mother energy, be it our Mom's or Mother Earth's.

Throughout our lives, our willpower choices suffer until we address childhood issues ranging from real or imagined betrayal to physical or emotional abandonment. We must tend to ourselves like a loving mother to her child. The clearing and healing of childhood issues is the beginning of psychological-emotional maturation. It is a re-parenting process that is vital to our ongoing spiritual transformation. Depending on the extent of damage, professional counseling may be needed before we integrate this center's self-nurturing energy fully.

Our charge as consciously evolving adults is to have already addressed or to begin to address early childhood development issues. Dysfunctional family-of-origin environment is an unfortunate global normality. Residue issues from childhood through young adult experiences vary in degree depending on each human's individual family setting. Mild imbalances can be easily addressed through self-growth commitments to study, learn and explore a new resonant psychology beyond familial dysfunctions. Extreme dysfunction in early developmental stages, ranging from alcoholic or addict parentage to excessive physical or emotional abuse or violence, are best met and addressed with professional therapeutic support as well as regular attendance in support group environs. In such spaces, we may recover connection with our inner resourcefulness and begin the journey back to healthy development of our thought-emotion energy processes.

We Carry Our Homes on Our Backs

Once we leave our first nest and head out into the world, we bring with us family-of-origin beliefs, habits and patterns of behavior. When they seem helpful (i.e., in service of our need to relate and support our basic human needs), we most likely continue the outward expression of those beliefs and patterns. When we realize them as dysfunctional, derailing our ability to move ahead in life, our evolving self will acknowledge minor to extreme imbalances and make the powerful choice to leave behind beliefs, habits and behaviors that no longer serve us. Stage One maturation empowered by open upper chakra energies helps us to decide which "tribal" values, be they familial or societal, are authentic to us. We go on to revisit our allegiances and loyalty, choosing to develop a personal moral code that we apply in all interactions with others.

First stage energy is our **connectivity** with all of life's people, places and the world at large. Governments, communities, justice, laws of order are all first-chakra related. What shapes our opinions and fears—of other nations, races, and religions different from our original family or groupings—may initially reflect adapted opinions and prejudice. These too are reexamined as we grow and ground our spiritually inclusive sensibilities. Once fully grounded in first-chakra energy, we are inspired by openness of upper chakras to have higher perspectives and conscious connection with Source energy.

Our quest is to learn to support our Self-recovery process, to honor our right to feel safe and secure as a participant in life. The "root significance" of a healed first chakra becomes apparent when honored as the foundation of our life. Whatsoever we were taught, and whatsoever we absorbed and adapted to regarding our basic survival needs when information was distorted, it all presents as fear-based behavior patterns that disrupt the stability of our daily life.

Understanding the Fear Response

Psychological fear, different from instinctual reality-based response, is this center's potential demon. Until our fear reaction is tamed with a commitment to understanding our individual psychology and engaging in conscious awareness practices we are its powerless servant. Fight-or-flight syndrome is part of our cellular biology, a primordial protective instinct programmed into humankind's physical evolution. We no longer run from saber-toothed tigers, yet at times we react from this basic instinct with "knee jerk" reactivity to simple, everyday occurrences.

We need our instinctual response when faced with real physical dangers. When first stage energy is out of balance, we react to simple situations, such as a misplaced cell phone or lost house keys, with unreasonable, frantic fear. We do the same in response to life circumstances that challenge or threaten our security like job loss or "basic needs" prosperity.

Unconscious triggers that mirror an unfounded belief that our life is in grave danger are acted out and drain our vital energy and resourcefulness. **Learning to relax and trust life is the spiritual challenge of this chakra.** Our quest toward its openness requires maintenance and attending to acceptance of its potent energy offering.

Ways to Open the Root

Grounding balanced physical movement (e.g., Hatha yoga, tai chi and dance) strengthens the first chakra's connection with Stage Seven vital 'presencing' energy (prana/breath) and grounds our roots. To aid in the return to a balanced chakra, walks in nature and connecting with earth's rooted solidity—while receiving energy from the sun, are all helpful practices. Our goal is learning to be in our bodies with conscious awareness and acceptance of our individual life. This is all about our right to be here on the planet, self-responsible, grounded and capable of standing on our own two feet.

Embracing the Fear of Change

When familial dysfunctional patterns taint our adult behaviors, our spiritual direction is to address then unflinchingly. Coping mechanisms related to fears of loss or abandonment may be wrecking havoc in our physical world. Deficient root chakra energy displays as anxiety, lack of discipline, financial difficulties and chronic disorganization. Addictive or compulsive relationships with food, work and money may be creating deficit energy in our body-temple's health as well as the relative balance of our bank account.

The only way to become unstuck is to face the nature of our fear and begin our way through—toward change. Change is scary and may for a while exacerbate our fears. They must be met 'heart' on as we stand upon our courageous willingness to change. Seeking the necessary support systems as we recover our ground *begins* to access our fourth chakra energy of self-love. (We will discuss this further in the Fourth Life Process.)

Psychological fear is mind-emotion's "thought form" energy. It stems from an unfounded belief that something is wrong, that something bad is going to happen. It will stop us in our tracks of recovering our sense of healthy boundaries and moving forward in life. Healing hidden fears creates opportunities of bonding with others as well as honoring our tribal identity and owning our personal power. The openness and flow of first-chakra energy concurs with the betterment of our interrelatedness within family and groups. Learning the art of belonging in life, with all its varied forms of relatedness, is something we all desire.

Meeting Our First Chakra Challenges

Our Stage One energy challenge is learning to access a relaxed state of body-mind awareness. Our commitment to working through our fear stems from our desire for a good life. Thusly, embracing a broader perspective in life becomes a core value. We consciously work to change our fear-based programming as an access point to feeling better about ourselves. Our intrinsic drive to evolve calls forth our willingness to develop individual choices based on our desire to become conscious and grounded.

Many of us feel a sense of disloyalty when embarking upon changes that dismantle tribal beliefs and patterns of thinking. As we begin to form opinions of our own, our developed personality's viewpoint may be in conflict with our parentage. We may acquiesce or rebel, depending on our sense of independence and self-reliance. This break from parental authority may appear as a stalemate love/hate encounter until mutual respect of divergent beliefs is acknowledged and hopefully accepted.

Our developmental challenge is to sort through the collection of inherited beliefs and decipher for ourselves which ones are harmful and which are worthy of our acceptance. This study, in contrast, gives rise to our continued individuation as we make our way out into the world experimenting with our personal code of ethics and worldview beliefs. With root energy in balance, we are able-bodied to choose individual beliefs beyond the inherently contradictive nature of family of origin and worldly influences.

While examining our beliefs, we become seekers of deeper meanings of truth beyond what we were taught as children and young adults. The beginning of these changes effectively creates a domino effect. Once we begin loosening the hold tribal belief had on us, we gain freedom to reassess our careers, attitudes, thoughts, ideas and our personal evolution's trajectory.

Here we ground ourselves able to honor renewed beliefs and healthy habits as we grow in spiritual personal power. Fulfillment of our first chakra's basic security needs is reflective of our matured proactive choice-making. Our body along with the body of our life circumstances is supported during every evolving stage along our path. Mastery of Stage One lessons means we have recreated our relationships with the physical aspects in our life. Alongside our physical body and our personal environment, group interactions become grounded with this center's open energy flow. By working through Stage One's challenges, we have supported our transformative journey from the ground up!

Personal relationships (second and fourth chakra), self-esteem (third), self-expression (fifth) and insightful wisdom (sixth) flourish when our roots are firmly planted. Once our body-temples have claimed solid ground, rains come winds blow and we respond with the intuitive heart power of our fourth chakra. Our spiritual centers' higher consciousness (sixth and seventh) supports our first-chakra responsibility of examining our basic survival fears. We learn to stand on our own two feet steady and stable. We walk the world unafraid of imaginary demons and dragons that once singed our mind with the fires of fear.

This is the lifelong journey we came here to embark upon. Whosoever our parentage, social groups, professional colleagues or friends, they are our evolutionary community. From the moment we are an embryo to vertical adulthood, our life experiences are what we came here to be with. Letting ourselves grow up spiritually—Self-empowered to choose our own values, perspectives and preferences.

And discover the courageous willingness to embrace change—that is our greatest strength.

Stage One Self- Inquiry

**Enjoy some full, deep, long...Inhales...Releasing
your breath with a focused Exhale...Give yourself
as many conscious breaths as you choose...**

**Take a moment, if you like, to settle
into a comfortable environment.**

~ Which of my basic human needs feel threatened at this time in
my life?

~ What "fight or flight" fear-based reaction do I "act out" most
often?

~ What is my understanding or concept of family? Who or what is my family at this time in my life?

~ How do I maintain my relationship with my family of origin or my extended family?

~ What compelling outer events are broadcasting a need for inner change?

~ Am I willing to ask for appropriate help, when needed, even if contrary to my "rules"?

~ What patterns of familial beliefs have I adopted as my own?

~ Which of these are no longer valid and empowering?

~ Which of these would I like to strengthen and develop?

~ How do I allow habitual belief patterns to dis-empower my personal authority?

~ Am I willing to ask for appropriate help when needed? If not, what pattern of belief limits me?

~ What societal laws of order govern my life? Which do I resist or break most frequently?

~ How does this affect my basic survival needs? What would I like to do differently?

Friendly reminder, the Micro Moves tool is always available to support discovery of your next step.

INTEND CREATE

Trust others

and they will be true to you.

Treat them greatly,

and they will show themselves great.

RALPH WALDO EMERSON

Second Inspiration

I had written a soliloquy of wisdom-truth on compassion in an attempt to offer inspired guidance.

About the fact that we are all going to die. That real death is ego dying. Spirit goes on forever. And so on.

It felt intellectualized.

Though, I met truth through sheer experience, how would I compassionately convey it?

I got up, put on my drawstring Champion shorts and a T-shirt from a Palau dolphin dive experience, planning to walk up in Wild Wood Canyon to clear my heady thinking...with Heart.

I paused and sat back down, cross legged in my bedroom's meditation space. I breathed for a moment.

Then I got up, saying to myself, "Okay, let's go." I stopped at my bedside table, don't remember what for. And there sat evidence of a simple truth. The one I'd tried to grasp at with my intellectual mind.

The day before a trip to the water store delivered more than alkaline H2O.

Sometimes spirit speaks through my mouth. During yesterday's refill task it showed me its mysterious Way. I greeted the East Indian shopkeeper with "Namaste," as he accepted my empty 3ml container.

He was a new face at our neighborhood watering hole. His personal nature is light and service oriented. We chatted about the goodness of life and God. When I passed over three dollars and change, he looked up at the ceiling with reverence. "I want to remember God," he said, with devotion on his face for a faraway Master.

Oh, I see. My pre-conceptions had slipped onto our experience. I assumed that he was Buddhist or Hindu based on his outer appearance. Maybe he is a faithful Christian.

A spontaneous heartfelt response from me opened his face. Gently, eye-to-eye, I spoke these words over the counter.

"We remember God when we look at Others and see God in them."

He seemed almost startled. On an out breath, a look of recognition lit up his face.

I was sparked as well. Energized as truth I knew, but sometimes forget, flew from my lips. In that moment, I recognized the presence of spirit.

Response-ability caused a desire to write the words down—'now', and I did. I nodded a smile to my new friend.

I wanted to jot down the exact message. I dismissed mind interference. A quick rummage in the car, a Walgreen's receipt for contact lens solution was the recipient of a spontaneous truth. I went so far as to indicate its section in the book. It wasn't this one. Ha! I laughed at my little mind's thinking.

Next morning after waking, I intended to impart words on compassion. Prayer meditation and writing practice brought me back to the ground. The simple truth I had found on my bedside table on a slip of paper that rested under a precious quartz heart stone, was the folded Walgreen receipt, with its misappropriated section number.

Spirit message received soft and clear. Once again it reminds me:

Being hurried, thinking we know, is a simple form of violence—even when couched in a holy mission. Thomas Merton, a seventeenth century Christian mystic, said as much—and more:

> *"The rush and pressure of modern life are a form,*
> *perhaps the most common, form of violence.*
> *It destroys our capacity for inner peace—it destroys*
> *the fruitfulness of our own work—because it*
> *kills the inner wisdom that makes work fruitful."*

Merton's wisdom words reflect our world's universal challenge. There's a way through. When we *listen* deeply, Being with *all-that-is...* slow down and watch the light shine, we notice it shines out from within us.

We walk out into the world lighting up smiles on the faces of strangers. We remember to say, feel and think *Namaste*: "The Divine in me honors the Divine in you."

I had joyfully laughed light tears—witnessing my little mind's attempt at co-opting Spirit's generous gifts.

A smile arose—with appreciation for the Way of authentic truth.

Namaste, sisters and brothers. A lyrical blessing from Hatha yoga gatherings:

"May the long-time sun...shine upon you. All love surround you. May the pure Light within you...guide you on...guide you on."

These days, I am occasionally drawn away from what I am doing—by neighborly hummingbird sounds. Their tiny wings vibrating, then **still**—discovering Life's sweetness. I'm fascinated, gently reminded to slow down---pause.

And b r e a t h e

All is well. We are loved.

Affirmation offering: *"I embrace not-knowing. I remain curious. I follow my Heart's wisdom."*

I'm b a a a a c k...

Due to intermittent loss of conscious memory, much of following details were gathered from family, friends, practitioners and medical records.

I was ambulanced back to St. Joseph's emergency department. Hospital records dated June 8, 2007, stated:

"The plan is for neurologic, rheumatologic and cardiac consultation."

~Dr. Taback–Cardio Pulmonary – primary physician

"I asked her about circumstances around loss of consciousness and she does not remember."

~Dr. Wonil Lee, rheumatologist (I have no memory of this interview)

Dr. Lee continues his report:
"She has slow cognitive function and decreased short-term memory." He suspected central nervous system vasculitis (inflammatory destruction of blood vessels) and added cautionary notes regarding medication management.

"The patient is awake, alert to person and place, but not time. She had speech difficulty, paraphasia (loss of ability to speak correctly) consistent with expressive aphasia. Poor memory. Poor concentration. Residual quadriparesis (neurological weakness in arms and legs). The patient does not remember anything that happened to her lately. Accordingly she needs evaluation for seizures."

~Dr. Sergey Akopov, Neurologist (I have no memory of this interview)

Three days after readmittance into St. Joseph's, I had almost stabilized enough for transfer to an acute rehabilitation unit. Dr Michael Lupo, the doctor in charge of the state-of-the-art Acute Rehabilitation Unit located on 5 North, was called in for consultation.

His June 11 report stated:

"The patient has multiple problems, including impaired mobility, impaired activity of daily living, cognitive issues and swallowing issues. Based on recent therapy documentation, patient is not tolerating sufficient therapy activities to meet criteria for acute rehabilitation admission. The patient will be followed on the acute floor for now."

He went on to say, "If patient were able to tolerate more intensive therapies we would certainly recommend admission. However we may need to consider less intensive level care, such as transitional care unit or a skilled level program. With goals focused on improving patient's mobility and self-care status—to a point she can return home or to an assisted-living-type of setting with supervision or minimal assistance."

There was hope. Though, I was still in poor condition.

I vaguely remember working with Cheryl, an occupational therapist, and Caroline, a physical therapist as well. After a few weeks I was transferred to the Transitional Care Unit (TCU). It was late June 2007.

I remember being inordinately depressed. The TCU environment was populated with patients ready to make their transitions, permanently.

I was forever blessed again. On July Fourth, the hospital chaplain, D'vorah Esptein-McDonald, came to visit me, a newly admitted patient whose Jewish surname caught her attention. D'Vorah Epstein, who has over the years become a dear friend, shared her recollection of that initial meeting.

The nurse, with my permission, allowed her to view the tailbone-area wound. She recalls being somewhat shocked and wondered silently: "How could someone's body have *that* and still be alive?" Accumulated wound photos from medical records substantiate her wonderment. I finally "got the picture," myself.

Reportedly, later that evening I had frantically asked nurses to call D'vorah. I must have wanted some peaceful guidance. She had finished work for the day. Gone home. Everything changed overnight.

I see who?…in I.C.U.

"The patient, after transfer from two weeks in Acute floor, was sent to TCU and doing fine apparently, until yesterday. This morning the patient developed acute hypertensive state and was feverish. The rapid response team was activated and performed fluid resuscitation. The patient was transferred to the intensive care unit. Her blood pressure is still low at 85/69.

She has a fever of 100.4 degrees she is awake but not communicating. Not participating in the examination."

~Dr. Sergey Akopov, Neurologist

I drifted in and out of coma for two months, being fed and medicated intravenously. A house of cards—secondary seizures, respiratory failure, kidney failure, pneumonia—plus life-threatening pressure wounds left me in a comatose dilemma. Spirit held the trump.

Dr. Taback e-mailed a reply to my 2011 request for family-friends-practitioners' recollections. "Must have told your family to expect you not to survive three times during your ICU stay." He added a great doctor note: "Thankfully you proved me wrong!"

Regina recalls having concerns about me ever being fully functional again after the exacerbated trauma my system experienced. Prayer and meditation circles, in multiple time zones, added my name. D'vorah remembers very clearly her daily visits. She stood and prayed over me. "Antoinette, know that you are in a deep conversation with God. This is the time you are making a decision."

We have laughed over brunch as we both acknowledged I was not making a hasty decision. I certainly took my time.

Nate and I walked St. Joseph's as I prepared to write this book. He remembered the door outside ICU where he met my older sister. "Yeah, Theresa said it looked like you weren't going to make it—and it was okay for me to go in and say my goodbyes."

Nate was asked to prepare a eulogy. After his ICU farewells, he joined his basketball team for their regular Thursday night game. He remembers toasting my life and commiserating with his dad. They sat at the team bar with beers, while Nate disbelievingly jotted down recollection notes.

Theresa, a former nurse turned teacher, snuck into ICU post visiting hours. She knew hospital drill. "Granny Goose . . ." she whispered to my intubated self. "It's Fuzzy Wuzzy— please come back."

My younger brother Joseph` sent an e-mail from Seattle, legally unable to leave Washington at the time. "Antoinette, I would like you to stick around, if you can. I think the world could really use you on this side of the existence plane. If you are given the choice to make a full recovery or graduate, please stay. I feel selfish to ask this but so be it. All my Love."

Jennifer Dunne, a long-time friend and colleague, flew in from her New Orleans film location. She had recently experienced her dad's stroke events. Jenn's one-word classic response when hearing I was on the edge in ICU: "Unacceptable." Doctors had asked family to invite familiar voices to visit and talk to me. When Jenn ran out of things to say, which isn't easy for Jenn, she read the newspaper. Her Mom, Sunny, had brought a book they read from as well. Jennifer felt I blinked or responded in some way, and enthusiastically reported her observations to ICU nurses.

Pause Your Mind Meditation in Venice, California, included my name and circumstances on their prayer list. The center was founded by Linda Neaman Lee, MA, Spiritual Psychology, who shared her memory of that time: "While you were in coma I received regular updates from Carmen (who had added my name) so we could adjust our prayers to fit your changing status. The organic process of prayer is heartfelt, so we continued to tune into our hearts and ask what you needed." Linda intuitively listens to her heart (fourth chakra energy) before she creates prayers for circle. She added, "Any prayer is good, but prayer that comes from heart energy goes much farther, deeper than rote prayers from the mind. Prayers from heart will be far more effective."

Carmen, who works as a childbirth educator (doula), yoga teacher and has an integrative body work practice shared, "Ardice had called and said, 'If you want to see Antoinette before you go to France, you'd better come now and say goodbye.'" This was early August 2011. Carmen continued, "I heeded Ardice's call. I knew—from working with Compassion in Action, a group that works with people making their transition, and knowing you had a lot of friends coming who were holding onto to you—that most likely no one was holding space---giving you permission to go. I remember saying to you, 'It would be okay. You are loved.' I told you I would be sad and miss you, but said if your Spirit needed to be freed from your body then that's okay. Regardless of what the doctors said, I never believed you would go—it just wasn't characteristic of who you are."

Michael (older brother) and Regina (younger sister) took turns being in town, staying in my Burbank condo. They managed all my various banking, incoming mail and Mexico property rentals. It would be several years before I regained cognitive skills, enough to manage my own finances. Regina and I later laughed at my uber-organized filing system. She said they felt fortunate to be able to access account information and records with such ease.

Donna blogged about her and Wendy's visit: "It was a shock to see this vital-funny-energetic woman laid up strapped down with tubes, connected to a monitor. Hooked up to life support in an ICU."

Donna goes on, "We'd spent a few minutes talking to her as doctors and family had requested. No response. Then the monitor started beeping loudly. Mindful that our friend's last visit had resulted in a loss-of-oxygen alert, we flagged down a nurse. When our friend finally reacted, it was not the way we were told she might. Michael had said she might open her eyes. This reaction was more disturbing. Her chest started to heave and tears rolled down her cheeks. Seeing her like this was shocking. The prognosis was frightening."

Donna, a mother and wife, radically changed her health regime and dropped 56 pounds after this experience. Deciding to be proactive about maintaining her good health.

Nurses who had met me on 5 North's Acute Rehabilitation floor were told they could come say their goodbyes. An interview with Cynthia Mascott, 5 North's Clinical Recreation Department head at that time, remarked: "After leaving our unit, we thought you might not make it, but were shocked and saddened at how rapidly you declined. We were very fond of you, even though you'd only been with us a short while. You still had a lot of life force in you. If you had died, it would have been too soon."

Another Chance

Nathan remembers my comatose state. "At times your eyes would open while still on the ventilator. You couldn't speak, but we knew you recognized us," he told me.

Carmen recalled, "When I saw you in the ICU, you were pure, simple grace. Lying there so still, so neutral, without judgment or expectation. Then once you began to awaken, being weaned off the ventilator, you couldn't talk. You were unable to communicate with your nurse when you needed something. In the smallest of movements, it was so beautiful to see how graceful you were in your patience."

It didn't last. But it was a start.

I still contained a willfully resistant ego-mind. After the March hospitalization, its habitual belief that it was in control nearly ended my earthbound days. Unflinching self-inquiry work was needed. Unraveling conditioned mental-emotional thought forms of self-destructive patterns waited. First I had to physically recover from ego's pitiful tug-of-war with Source, with all of my Heart.

Ego violence took me to the edge. The near disintegration of my body was an initiation. This generously humbling rite of passage experience would guide me home. Home: a *pathway toward integration* of a healthy ego-personality led by a soulful heart. The road I'd always wanted to travel. My invitation had arrived.

Spirit orchestrated a dynamic unfolding that was perfect for me. It broke open my stubborn mind and reclaimed my true heart. It left me in pieces, like a Humpty Dumpty, fallen off the same illusive brick wall that had imprisoned my heart. No-thing, no one could put me together; they could only wait and watch.

Appreciative honoring has been extended to all the medical practitioners, clinicians and therapists who waited and watched. Their expert actions and choices aided and upheld the workings of an Invisible force that had brought me back to life.

Family, friends and others I've yet to meet sent visible and invisible requests to whatever Higher Power was in their hearts. Love answered prayers. Powerful Compassion—a primordial Force greater than a reactive resistance I had within my mental programming— returned me to my body.

Krishnamurti simplified years of wisdom teaching when asked about his secret to enlightened living: ***"I don't mind what happens."***

I had been stuck in the mind's minefield of seriously minding what happens. I said I wanted to know God. My prideful self had to be brought to its knees. Source's redemptive grace invited me back for another chance.

Second Life Process

Stage Two energy's life lessons include partnership and relationship interdependency. How we relate with one another and life. Our individual needs for safety and physical security rely on our ability to relate with others. We participate in an interdependent world environment. Second-chakra energy empowers us to participate in life with patience, endurance and our intrinsic well-being.

Our second chakra houses our vital energy. It is our energy-bank center located below our navel above our pubis region. It is our lower-level energy center of instincts. Our instinctual energy center exists in our sexual organs, pelvis, hips, kidneys, bladder adrenal glands, prostate plexus and female reproductive system.

As youngsters, we rely on stage-one tribal authority for safety and protection. As adults our ability to maintain relationship skills is developed. This earthy powerful energy connects us to a state of healthy, balanced self-management in regard to our interactions with others. It energizes our ability to self-determine where we end and others begin.

As we grow beyond dependency on familial material support, we take responsibility for our needs. Our first-chakra tribal energy splits into a dual nature. Our individual growth now dictates how we succeed out in the world. By early adulthood if steady growth continues, we are able to relate effectively with others. As we mature to collaboratively cooperate with others, we create and nurture opportunities for self-sufficiency. We also self-determine what is most needed to sustain our status quo.

The energy of this stage governs our ability to interact with external forces. Our life lessons are related to our power of choice. Second-chakra energy shifts and expands respective of age. Its balance or imbalance reflects the measure of control we have within external life situations.

The Rise of Creative Energy and Power

The choices we make with Stage Two's personal creative power reflect our growing consciousness. A deepened understanding of the interdependence inherent in partnership-relationship success is respected. Whether in personal or business associations, our goal is to learn discernment of choice. Careers, homes and children all require relationship. Second-chakra energy empowers our ability to choose appropriate partners, friends and business relations.

Stage Two offers a powerful charge of grounded, lower instinctual creative energy. It is distinctly different from inspired creativity, a seventh-chakra promise. Here in our seed center of creativity, we create at a physical level. Chakra two fuels our ability to financially provide for ourselves and contribute to relationship or family of our own. We are becoming confident to take risks. Energy reliability of this chakra strengthens fulfillment of our stabilized-security needs. Our willingness to ask and listen for Invisible assistance brings clarity to this dance. We advance when inner growth becomes a priority value.

Our personal power is expressed through our relationship with sexuality, morality and creativity, as well as money matters. Higher Source infused power is our life-force energy. A disconnect with our spiritual life force manifests as imbalanced personal power. Our relationship with authority, other people, money and sexuality grows as we create and respect our healthy boundaries.

Relative to our second chakra's open-balanced state, we experience an attraction to physical forms of power: materialism, ownership, possession, mental-emotional-physical addiction, authority and control issues. These may be mildly active, or they may dominate our experiences.

Second chakra energy empowers us to recover from loss and bounce back when external circumstances change. We may have formed a healthy ego, able to remain objective about the ongoing change life presents. Our Stage Two challenge is to reach maximum achievement-accomplishment with life goals. Our personal definition of "maximum achievement" shifts and changes as our consciousness expands. Ideally we become capable of releasing reactive worry or fear when situations do not turn out according to our plan.

When we react fearfully to change, it is indicative of Stage Two energy issues: a need for control—or fear of being controlled. An unconscious need to control people places and things may be hidden behind a depressive disappointment. Anger, frustration and fear can be triggered if our expectations are denied, until we develop this energy's intended use of power.

We consciously evolve to trust in the powerful flow of life, knowing it is *for us* and will meet our every need. Once we recognize and accept our true Nature, we surrender an immature ego's need to control. Our second chakra energy's spiritual quality assists us in releasing what is no longer viewed as a necessity in life. The challenge for us is to develop higher perspectives. Intentionally discover a renewed interpretation of what 'necessity' means.

Recognized authentic intent empowers us to move out into life in a consciously creative manner. What fuels our intention is paramount to its outcome. Conscious presence helps us maintain awareness of our motivations. It is imperative to recognize what is behind, inside and around any creative intention we undertake. Conscious awareness knows intent is the key energy that creates outcomes.

Knowledge that our intentions affect us as well as those around us reflects *inspired* second-chakra energy (empowered by opening of upper chakras). This center represents "no one is an island" when it comes to activating results out in the world. We grow in respect of this universal principle as our consciousness expands.

Our personal ethics and morals develop as this center flourishes and grows. Our intentions maximize to include a highest good for all concerned. We notice that commitment to healthy communion with others strengthens our personal and group productivity.

Conscious Choice and Sexuality

Second chakra's balanced or imbalanced state is revealed through our power of choice. Our choice-making grows as this center opens. Wisdom or unawareness is demonstrated through our life choices and flexibility with change. The inner recognition and alignment with a power greater than ourselves shifts our lower energy reactivity to a higher perspective of the power of choice. Our choices evolve to be of an inspired-intuitional nature. We begin to be with personal choice as a sacred trust. How we *be* with what we *do* models a higher consciousness of what choice truly means.

Our promises and commitments with others operate within this chakra center. Our choices reflect our ethics and morals as we decide what is acceptable or unacceptable in relationship-partnership experiences. Second chakra energy transmits signals via *instinctual sensations* when we behave in a manner less than our personal code of honor.

Our elemental sexual nature reverberates in second chakra's energy. It is our co-creative kundalini energy that reunites us with divinity. It is our inborn nature to want balanced yin-yang: male-female energy experiences. No matter our sexual preference, this dualistic energy dance wants to be satisfied. Until we connect with a Higher Beloved, our energy can be tainted with distorted understanding of human mating rituals.

Early stages of a base animal magnetism, a lower consciousness state, may dominate our interactions with sexual partners. When a need for control or power is active, an expression of seductress-seducer behavior may show up in our personal or professional life, fulfilling little more than the desire for sexual entertainment. Using our seductive-erotic nature to demean our sacred sexual nature is a dysfunctional form of control.

Extreme imbalance of second-chakra energy appears as destructive disrespect of self or others. Acts of control and the misuse of power in our sexual realm include rape, incest and adultery. As we grow into our spiritual nature, we leave power plays behind, give up seductive manipulative behaviors, and relinquish our need to control or be controlled. We choose to allow our energy to flow naturally. Honoring an innate sexual-sensual drive arises as our conscious awareness opens. We no longer need to politically motivate people or partners to like us. A quality of matured third chakra energy begins to emerge: self-esteem.

Trust in relating arrives when we connect with our primary relationship. The Invisible force that created us eons ago is our inner Sacred Beloved. We spiritually realize we are never alone. We cease being needy clingy or controlling. Once we honor the truth that our true happiness rests inside, we let go of thinking it can be derived from another. We become capable of genuine relating. Partnerships become sacred relationships once we gain ground in second chakra energy. Ultimately intimate expressions are shared to further our never-ending evolution.

We re-evaluate *where we are* and *where we want to go*, based on our evolving state of consciousness. We ask ourselves "What is true outer world achievement?" and discover our own definition of accomplishment. We experiment and discover through experience what resonates, positively or negatively. From this self-empowered space, we evaluate what gives us an inner sense of fulfillment.

Our answers shift as we spiral through stages, change and grow, continually revisiting and renewing our perspective.

The paradox of Stage Two energy's impetus is: it pushes us forward while we simultaneously learn we are not ultimately in control. We grow to develop an ability to give up our intellect's angst. Further, we become strengthened to act from prudence and patience in our daily living. When we are unattached to the outcome of our plans, the more we trust the flow of life.

The Dawn of Surrender

We learn to act from a place of surrender, yielding to *what is*, recognizing the only control we have is conscious awareness of our mental-emotional state. Our ability to cooperate with the flow of Life signals our returned connectivity with Higher Intelligence. It guides us to understand our responsibility in creation-manifestation of outcomes.

Until we grow a conscious awareness of our mind-emotion disposition's energetic frequency, we are in a state of vacillation and flux with matters of control. Our attempts at control dissipate our vital energy. Anxiety may result. Second-chakra blockages appear as addictive attachments, not only in matters of money and sex, but in all areas of our physical needs and desires. If this energy center is out of balance to the extreme, we relate with unconscious disrespect of our life and others. Second-chakra energetic imbalance also reflects humanity's worst forms of the disempowering need for control.

Addiction to alcohol, health-harming narcotics, work-a-holism and other compulsive-obsessive self-destructive behaviors are second-chakra energy issues. Personal power choices that deplete our resources and energy, including shop-a-holism and co-dependency in relationships, may be active until we spiritually mature.

The lesson inherent in this center is a learned respect within all external relations. Attention to how, where, when and why we make the choices we do, as well as who we consider when we make them, reveal to us our earlier formed unconscious habits. Habitual behaviors are founded on unexamined concepts and reactive beliefs. We want to consider what habits are impeding or advancing our personal spiritual growth.

When we commit to healing our psycho-spiritual issues (alone or with a counselor), our inner work acts as an agent that reconnects us with Source. We recognize that a power greater than our little mind supports our heartfelt moves forward in life. We learn to live a day at a time, trusting our connection with Invisible energy inside us. We begin to strengthen our third-chakra energy of self-esteem as well.

Once we gain ground with our inner work (i.e., complete what we need to complete and leave the past behind) space opens for new energy to charge our purer motivations and intentions. Our respect and integrity invites higher levels of visible and Invisible support. We release a dependency for outer events to make us feel good. We become responsible for our genuine happiness.

When we recognize the fundamental truth of our deservingness to feel good, without use of outer stimulus, we welcome divine intervention into our daily living. As we shift, our energy opens; we attract the *exact* person or circumstance necessary for our further opening. We become aware that whoever we relate with is a teacher, a reminder of some aspect of ourselves that wants to blossom or die.

Our Energetic Template for Relationships

Underdeveloped second-chakra energy displays as a victim complex. Guilt and blame oriented thoughts words or actions would be present and are likely directed at oneself, others or both. As we open our heart center, through learning the art of forgiveness, we realize each of us is doing the best we can from wherever we are in consciousness.

The second chakra in unison with fifth stage's communicative energy equalizes our self-expression regarding all others. When closed, thoughts emoted with negative opinions of others and our self may cause comparative or competitive reactions. During this stage's development, an imbalanced ego personality dictates (or permits) us to cheat, steal or gossip; these are examples of extreme misuse of our Stage Two creative energy. Here we may find ourselves disrespecting of self, others and what is theirs.

As we spiritually mature, we create meaningful relationships with externals that reflect our consciousness. We let go relationships (of all kinds) that detract from our intentional expansion. Our personal power expands with spiritual confidence. We become capable of authentic awareness of others' qualities and uniqueness. Freed from competitive and comparative thought-emotions, we easily extend honest acknowledgement to others, when appropriate.

Source empowers us and infuses our courage to change. When our conscious awareness is connected with Its support we feel empowered to let go of behaviors that no longer reflect who we are becoming. We recognize the loss of precious energy in power plays or seductive behaviors and choose authentic relatedness with others.

We grow with our commitment to introspective practices that reveal our unique interpretation of a deeper meaning of life. Our matured second-chakra energy unites with upper centers' spiritual energy. Our improved relatedness—with people, external desires, creative accomplishment, and the power of choice—reflects our higher consciousness.

Stage Two Self-Inquiry

**Enjoy some stillness. Inhaling fully and
exhaling deeply, allowing your deep breaths
to s l o w your body down as you
B r e a t h e... B r e a t h e... B r e
a t h e...Deeply and often...
Have as many as you choose...**

**Take a moment to settle into a
comfortable environment of choice.**

~ Where, if ever, in my life have I compromised my sacred sexual
nature? What motivated me? What would I choose differently
about this in the future?

~ What is my personal code of ethics? How do I express it in my interactions with others?

~ Would I describe myself as attached, addicted or unable to control my thoughts or behaviors? How do I use people, places or things as stimuli to feel in control in life? How does this affect my overall productivity?

~ What motivates my choices regarding work? What are my key intentions? What do I most want to create when interacting with others?

~ Would I describe my relationship with money as functional or dysfunctional? How does this affect the balance of my life's situations?

~ What Higher Power do I place my faith and trust in? Do I trust a God of fairness? Am I afraid I will be punished for immoral or less-than-best behaviors?

~ Do I ever feel willing to compromise myself in professional or personal relationships for monetary gain?

~ How do I provide for myself and family? What satisfies or dissatisfies me about my current ability to provide?

~ What is my definition of achievement? What would I like to accomplish that best describes my ideal achievement?

~ Am I influenced by the opinions or prejudices of others? How does this affect the choices I make?

~ What motivates and interests me about life? What, if any, fears do my interests stimulate?

~ Would I call myself a controlling person or do I feel a need to be controlled? What does this behavior cause in my relationships? In my personal and professional experiences?

~ What is the quality of my conversations with and about others? Are they sometimes cloaked in deception, gossip or negative intent? What motivates me to speak in a less-than-truthful manner?

~ Would I describe myself as competitive? How often do I compare myself and my achievements with others' accomplishments?

~ Have I prepared an Advance Directive so those who would mourn my transition are aware of my final wishes?

The Micro Moves tool is available to support discovery of your next step.

INTEGRITY IN~TU~ITE

Patience leads to

the power to practice...

Practice brings the

Grace that leads to

Liberation...

AML

Third Inspiration

How do we answer the call "To Thine own Self be True"?

"Know Thy Self" comes first. How do we learn Who We Really Are?

Nature's symbolic insights are our constant companions. They tell stories offering hints and clues.

The bear wisely hibernates. The butterfly's metamorphosis mirrors our own. The hummingbird effortlessly moves—forward, backward, sideways. It takes flight or stops, in an instant. Wings hum a figure eight's symbolic song of infinity.

Our transformative stages reflect nature's symbols. We learn to observe. Be meditatively present.

Incense glows hot. A candle flame flickers. Shadows reveal themselves in the dark.

Here we sit. In silence. The second-hand ticks, tracking time while we visit timelessness.

Hibernate daily in repose. Meet silent space. Allow stillness to quiet the limbs. Open the mind's eye.

Thoughts flood-flow-flit across the horizon in a past-future picture show. Watch. Observe.

Thunder claps, rain showers drizzle. Understand. Liquid love streams. Dampens our cheeks. Heart Mind Channels open. We are receptive…still…at peace.

Butterflies are born of egg. We arrive egg-embryo-fetus. We are cocoon-like in womb, where we are fed and grow effortlessly.

Next we emerge. Caterpillar confident. We learn to feed ourselves. Growing wisdom morphs and returns us. A chrysalis state is chosen, again. Our meditative inner growth's appearance—of lifelessness—contains movement. As we do what we must.

Watch process move on its own terms. Make time to be receptive. Allow life its course.

Adult butterflies emerge in the warmth of spring. This reflects our wizened choice ability…to sit in yielding surrender. To be with *what is.*

Now we are able to rise. Give wings to intentions of the day. Re-creation comes forth—from our natural light.

Our bear-like courage muscle has grown—
Our butterfly wings elevated by silence,
A sweet hum nurtures vibrantly.

Our inner beauty and strength witnessed. New horizons appear. Freedom is here.

We sit silently. And patiently wait. Imitating nature's cycles of birth-death-rebirth, day to day. We begin anew with deepened trust in our hearts.

Oh happy day. We real-ize our eternal, immortal, infinite Self-contains our beauty and strength.

"Leap of Trust": Awareness Exploration

Ask yourself, "What will be my answers, on my death bed, joyfully ready to make my transition?" What five aspirations have I fulfilled that allow me to depart in satisfied peace?"

Remembering, "I realize my answers change, shift, morph—throughout my evolving life. I update and honor my values as I change and grow."

Tenacious Miracle Child

Surgical tape secured a short plastic contraption. It itched. *"What is that? Where am I?"* was my fuzzy post-coma cognitive functioning. *"How did I get here?"* rattled around in my damaged brain. I felt terrified and afraid for my life. I had no idea of my serious flirt with disintegration. Or that the thing around my neck was a souvenir trach tube that supported access to air as my respiratory system came back to life.

I drifted in and out of wakefulness. Tubes, plastic lines and hoses were attached to my body, head to toe. With no conscious memory of being intubated, I was muddled, confused and thoroughly unable to function. Which meant acting "in control" was not an option. I depended entirely on others for every human need. A critical care ICU unit was unfamiliar territory. My body lay there, copiously medicated for acute pain and deadly infections.

My post-coma forwarding address was scouted with Nathan in 2011. We exited an elevator, using my medical records as a tour map. Nate noticed, "This is where I first visited you after ICU. It took a minute to realize that I had entered your room. Strapped into the bed, you had been attempting to tear out the IVs and leave. Thinking the doctors were trying to kill you. And there were armed gunmen as well. It was serious to you, but I was amused. You wanted me to get some scissors and help you escape." We enjoyed a soft chuckle, honoring the hospital's quiet.

"We had been concerned what the quality of your life would be, *if* you made it back. You were becoming aware of the enormity of recovery ahead. You began to recognize how debilitated you were. And that your life would be very different. It wouldn't be until much later that you realized just how close you were to going out—and how far you'd have to come—to come back."

I have memory slices of being restrained, strapped to a First Step Select specialty bed, unable to speak or see clearly or move, unaware of my body's damaged state or the extreme nature of measures I had taken to reconnect with Source. The First Step bed was intended to ease contact pain from head-to-toe open wounds. Its mattress overlay had regulated air inflation. On several memorable occasions it deflated. My tailbone touched down against a hard surface. I had no idea why excruciating jolts of pain assaulted my body.

Thank God for Dr. Taback's no-nonsense request at the sounds of my muted screams: "Replace this bed immediately, please." We went through several air-leak dramas until one became a temporary home base for months. Unrelenting bodily pain would be with me for quite a while.

On our tour, Nate mentioned that family and friends had continued to hold a collective breath during my post-ICU recovery stages. I had a very long way to go. He had enjoyed some humor remembering, "You thought you saw a rat or lizard." An absolute impossibility in the pristine sanitized hallways we walked through! My hallucination stories entertained many friends over time.

But there is one they still haven't heard…

While strapped down, I believed I was bleeding to death from between my legs, unable to save myself. I *think* I made attempts to get the nurses to come. But failed miserably because I was unable to call out or function enough to find and use the call button. I felt powerless. I remember with certainty and deep sadness that I would lay there and die. The illusionary bleeding I sensed was a wicked, stubborn case of C difficile (a bacterium that causes depletive diarrhea) that drained my body of nourishment for weeks. I became a medically declared involuntary anorexic. My body's muscular system was extremely weak and completely atrophied.

I dreamt of making warrior moves—fighting, running, hiding from drug cartel operatives that owned the hospital. Apparently I had witnessed their international drug dealings go bad and they meant to assassinate me. My bed railings were filled with hungry Egyptian scarabs, beetles symbolic of death and rebirth. A large blue E.T. stood in the corner of my room pointing up toward its way home. Multi-dimensional humans in hospital gowns floated passed my open door. Transparent beings with a serene turn of the head glanced in, smiled and went on their way.

Many holographic images flashed through my consciousness in weird and vivid succession. Their underlying death-rebirth-past-life metaphoric messages would eventually become clear. And serve as an open invitation to cross a threshold and return to the ethers.

My older brother listened to my fearful feelings about the drug cartel. He asked a simple question: "If they're so powerful, wouldn't they have gotten to you already?" Michael's gentle common sense helped. I considered it. It felt like a logical perspective. *"Aha!"* my confused brain lit up.

Many more lights were ahead. Red, yellow and green—as I became more receptive to my current reality.

In Nathan's opinion, I lived because: "You are tenacious. That's why you're here. What else were you going to do, roll over and die? You'd just fought to be alive."

During his first visit after ICU he observed, "You were too alive, though extremely debilitated, to give up. You were depressed and wanted to talk to someone spiritual, not religious."

I had no memory of meeting D'vorah back in early July. It would be a while before I recalled knowing her. Or realized how close I'd been to leaving. It would be weeks before I worked with therapist.

Family and friends followed me throughout my recovery, stage to stage, floor to floor, until I was readmitted to the Acute Rehabilitation Unit on 5 North. When I heard a familiar staff member refer to me as "the miracle child," I had no idea what she meant.

B r e a t h e....A Little Bit

When I was still horizontal, learning how to breathe—independently—was my first adult lesson. With the last two month's events entirely unknown to me, understanding waited. I began my work at coming back to life. Friends, family, and strangers visited with hopeful gratitude. A tentative sense of relief imbued the air. Loving "you're alive" gifts accumulated. Everyone held a collective breath, timid that another shoe would drop. People visited in variable waves. I stayed afloat. It took years to recognize these events had a strong psychological impact on loved ones. I had no recall of visitors in ICU, where Michael had regulated visitations.

He called me "Little Bit" when he visited regularly from San Diego. In my "before events" grand-personality life, this nickname would never have been used. I would later understand what "Little Bit" meant. I had finally been weaned off intravenous fluid supplements. Mike would help me eat when nurses weren't available. I still needed help being fed. Top-notch practitioners came and went. Doctors and nurses poked, prodded, checked and charted. Chaplin, psychologist and social worker counseled, and the therapist taught.

It was time to practice and learn—*relearn*—every voluntary bodily function. I was amazed at the existence and expertise of acute rehabilitation teams. And how they provide relearning support within and beyond hospital walls. Some sessions with this marvelous rehab team were cancelled, due to my exhaustion. Otherwise I eagerly engaged.

Red-haired Leslie Peterson, occupational therapist, came to my room twice a day. We started with early-life-skill's basics, including how to hold a spoon. At first I gripped it like a two-year-old and scooped at the liquefied food. Next I learned how to hold and balance it between my fingers. Then my brain had to regain connections to signal how to get the food up and into my mouth. I practiced shamelessly, often missing and spilling food all over my hospital gown.

In-room speech therapy began in earnest. Maya Highorany, clinical speech pathologist, tall, gorgeous hoot, came to my room. We'd met before apparently, but I didn't remember. To this day, I credit her expertise with jump-starting my cognition. I'd always been a talker. I was hungry to learn again, and to read and write. Reading books caused dizzy spells at this point. Though mathematics and homework on weekends were not my favorite, she has been unconditionally pardoned. Maya is a great humorist. She and several nurses particularly encouraged levity. We cracked up at my faulty efforts. It helped. Her eventual recommendation would relieve me of the trach tube. I had to learn how to swallow first. I choked a lot. I had this enormous appreciation for, and realization of, the importance of breath. It felt oddly unfamiliar, a jerky strangeness reconnecting with the inhale-exhale reflex. Dr. Taback eventually accepted Maya's recommendation. He approved and removed the rather uncomfortable, no-longer-required trach tube. It took a few years to not react in fear of suffocation, if a bed sheet or anything seemed to block access to free breathing.

This newfound appreciation for breathing led to recognition and deep respect for breath's connectivity with all of life. It reminded me of our microcosmic role in a macrocosmic system. I was an energy experiment in process. As my brain very slowly rebooted, teeny incremental techniques to reconnect it fully were progressed. Electromagnetic firings were gearing me up to play.

John Monroe, physical therapist, visited the room twice a day. It would be weeks before I was able enough for a wheelchair ride, fifty or so feet down the corridor to the rehab gym. I'd been stopped, for the first time in my life. I felt grateful for having time and space without outside responsibilities. Not have to do or be a productive person, for myself or anyone else. This was space I had never given myself before. I had no choice. It was a wonderful relief, for a while.

My first dream is still vivid. Dad, who transitioned in 1996, was behind the wheel of his favorite 1970s classic auto. He drove down a ramp into an underground parking garage, where I stood polishing a shiny new sports car. He never got out. I looked at him, so happy for the visit, wanting to talk. We said nothing. Love was present. He smiled and circled back up. Before he disappeared into the garage exit's well-lit opening, he turned and waved goodbye. Even in my drug-induced state of mind, I was consoled by his metaphoric visit.

Later, at times, I was inconsolable. Cynthia Mascott, M.S., Clinical Recreational Department head, called it chronic mood swings or getting up on the "wrong side of hospital bed" syndrome. No one could help. D'vorah visited. Nurses called the clinical social worker. My unpredictable tears flowed from a realization of loss. I was graduating beyond denial. Transitioning to grieving.

Regina, a master social worker in the area of bereavement, felt my pains. We talked on the phone about the monumental effort it would take for me to go on. In so many words, she expressed, "You don't have to try if you don't have it in you." I understood I had a conscious choice to make. I took it to heart and slept on it. The now familiar specialty bed did help ease incessant bodily pain. Hooked up to IVs, hoses and lines, I went to sleep. The next morning, like many to follow, I was still in pain, unable to rise or do anything for myself. Yet I managed to get on the hospital phone. "Regina," I said, "I want to live, no matter how much work it takes."

That was it. I chose to take a leap of faith. There must have been a sacred secret ICU agreement, a choice made in a split-second gap— *do you want to live or do you want to die?*—that was being honored.

My brain had rebooted just enough to know that I was clueless about every life function. Remember the initiatory feeling of relief that had settled over me? From not being expected to know how to do anything, or to how do it well? It was the beginning of surrender.

A new ability to *be with what is* was definitely in the making.

Vampires and Mirrors...LOL

Initially, I was terrified that I would never get out of that hospital bed, be able to walk, go to the bathroom, take a hot shower, or drive ever again.

A Wound VAC unit (drainage machine for the infected sacral wound), intravenous stand and catheter bag were my appendages on wheels once I graduated to rehab gym sessions. Wheeled there by John, P.T., I was shocked by the reflection I saw in the mirror. I was every "little bit" the spitting image of a very shrunken me. I asked John, "Will I ever walk again?" It was too soon for that question. We had a lot of work to do. And we did it, even though the first time I rose from the wheelchair, weeks later, to practice walking on the training bridge, I crashed into John. We both landed on the floor as he skillfully buffered any bodily harm.

One night, a while afterward, I had a predictive dream. I will never forget the *feeling* I *experienced* walking across an unfamiliar small kitchen. I was elated—it felt so real! With enthusiasm for the next day's sessions, I asked John what he thought about my symbolic kitchen scene. "Of course you will walk again, Antoinette, it will just take some time," he replied. And it did.

I arrived at a juncture where these experiences cracked open my previously underdeveloped sense of humor. Once I could talk, slur or stutter, I'd joke with the nurses. It's a daily routine to ask a patient their level of pain: "On a level of one to ten, how would you describe your pain this morning, Antoinette?" Like clockwork, high-caliber 5 North Acute Rehab nurses entered early and asked me this question.

"Is there an 'off the charts' score available?" I'd reply. We'd chuckle together. I wasn't Norman Cousins yet, but it was a good sign. Early morning lab techs, affectionately called "vampires," came for daily blood. One could set the clock by their visits, punctual and ready to puncture. A morning came when both arms' vessels were flat worn out. A nurse highly regarded for blood removal was called in from another floor. Her first few efforts failed. I waited and watched, breathing the best I could. I joked clumsily, unable to speak very clearly yet. Victory! Blood flowed. Morning sample collected.

Several in room visits per week with Dr. Richard Rogal, Ph.D., psychologist, lightened my mental heaviness, eventually to a point where I could laugh out loud at his verbal prescription: "You need to plan, to be more spontaneous." A slight New York accent lingered with his consolatory sessions. We chatted once about his attendance at the same elementary school as Woody Allen. I greatly appreciated Dr. Rogal's solid grounding and great sense of humor. Serendipity arrived during our heavy psychological efforts. A forgiving breakthrough happened while we discussed my 1989 divorce: I finally forgave myself for harmful dysfunctional relationship patterns.

Chaplain D'vorah's inner light "life-lined" my own. Her chaplain training included Jewish studies. During one of our sessions, she commented that my spiritual learning and leaning aligned with Kabbalah's mystical teachings. She might have, upon occasion, indulged my off-key singing. I don't remember, but I remember the spiritual songs I sang. One in particular resurfaced from Catholic school days: "Make me a channel of your peace." This melody, with words from St. Francis's prayer, helped me stay centered. Invoking lyrics from Agape Center of Truth kept trying to reboot and spill forth from my mouth. I could not remember all the words. "Mother–Father

God how great you are, how infinite, how wonderful" was the best I could do, at the time.

Cynthia and her team from Clinical Recreation pampered me, always treating me like a favorite return guest. They knew I would want a video player and movies to help me fall asleep at night.

Very seldom did I use the television or phone. I'd lose the call button, and the hospital phone confused me. I was not cognitively cell phone capable. Nurses were forever patiently recovering important cords and placing them in reach. Movement was always uncomfortable if not painful. Each night, the nurses placed pillows between my knees before I slept on my side in order to relieve the tailbone wound. The pillows also eased skin-and-bone-rubbing discomfort. Doctors wanted me to fatten up, insisting that I eat everything I wanted once taken off restricted medical meals. This was a new deal, as I had been self-consciously dieting my whole life since my pre-teens. I was hungry and ready to follow orders. I actually dreamt of a Double-Double with Fries, a special treat from California's well-known In-N-Out fresh fast-food chain. A nurse in my dream had helped me escape and go AWOL.

At times I felt like a well-cared-for prison inmate, a long-term bed-ridden hotel guest. Under strict doctor's orders, I never left the bed without a nurse or therapist's assistance. I was in learning mode with all basic living skills. Breathe, eat, drink, walk, talk were being taught—patiently, slowly, gently, step by step.

Finally, with John's assistance, I pushed myself up and out of a wheelchair, reached out one hand at a time, and balanced onto a walker. The feeling of standing up for the first time in three months remains an unforgettable moment. Many firsts were yet to come before I could go home. Providence Saint Joseph's team bridged my reentry. Adult learning was a profound experience.

Acute rehabilitation was an opportunity, a reintroduction to learn new and improved ways of doing basic living skills. It also taught me that micro-incremental steps would lead to accomplishing any result in my life.

It would be months more before I reclaimed any personal hygiene routines. Cynthia recalled, "I remember pictures of you with friends—you had all your hair. We thought 'she's actually kinda pretty.' You wouldn't have known by looking at you—you were a mess, eyes not in focus, balding hair loss, you looked awful." And unbeknownst to me, my teeth were a mold factory. None of this mattered in the least.

After several months, Cynthia wheeled me out to a hospital garden for the first time. Wearing the big straw hat she'd procured for me, I exclaimed, "Oh my God, I love this." I didn't know how much I'd missed being with green plants and blue sky. The sense stimulus was overwhelming. We had to go back inside. It would take some time to be okay with noise and light.

And though I dreamt of escape from hospitalization, I was also hospitalized. I'd become used to the hospital's protection and safety. By early September I was scared to go home.

I remained an eager, anxious adult student. My sense of humor was livening up. I was able to laugh at myself more and more often. Cynthia claims I had a sense of humor from day one. "It was just a little 'out there' for our conservative environment. You might have blown John's mind," she noted. If I did, he had been a good sport, always the consummate professional.

I was irritable with a few nurses. I knew I was. Cynthia acknowledged this. "You were kind of demanding," she commented. "I told one of the nurses you are a good person. I knew it from our private talks. 'Give her some time, she's in extreme pain,' I said."

She remembers watching a video of me doing an ET interview. I had location managed-associate produced Edward James Olmos's 1991 film *American Me*. Jessica had brought in a "behind the scenes" clip of our streetcar location. We shot the 1943 Los Angeles zoot-suit riot scene on Universal Studios' back lot. "It was fun to see and realize that you were lively and animated to begin with," remarked Cynthia. "It showed you when you could walk and talk. We had no reference point of what you looked or acted like before hospitalization. I also knew you weren't anywhere near giving up your profession. You watched the video repeatedly." Old habits die hard, indeed.

Horizontal Boogie

Horizontal boogie days would change my body's structure forever. Remember the sacral coccyx wound? It was still a medical threat. Dr. Taback, Dr. Lee and team had hoped I'd stabilized months ago. Wanting to address the urgency of the open tailbone pressure wound, Dr. George Orloff, a specialist in reconstructive surgery, had been called in for consultation. Here's a peek at a few of his August 2, 2007, notes:

"This 51 year old female is in the intensive care unit with severe post-stroke encephalopathy. The patient has a tracheostomy. She is being fed via central line using parenteral nutrition. Lupus is being controlled with high-dose steroids. She is recovering from exacerbation of renal (kidney) failure requiring dialysis. The patient has severe, altered mental state—does not respond to physical stimuli and does not respond to commands. Stage IV sacral decubitus ulcer. I do not consider the patient, currently, to be a surgical candidate."

Nearly two months after his report, Doctor Orloff visited me on 5 North. He found me on lunch break from therapy, in a wheelchair outside my hospital room. Nurses had set me up to eat over my rolling bedside table. It was in the midst of a late September therapy-filled day. I stopped to listen. The combined doctors' opinion: I was ready for the surgery. I called Dr. Wonil Lee from the nurse's station across from my room. He took the call. "We wanted this to happen in early August." It was almost October. That's all I needed to hear.

I'd take the surgical risk Dr. Orloff had outlined. There were various. The key failure threat was that my body would reject the muscle transplant. *"Management of massive stage IV sacral decubitus ulcer with anterior flap, hip disarticulation and myocutaneous gastrocnemius fillet flap"* meant that part of my right glute muscle needed to be moved onto my tailbone. The operation would begin closure of the open wound. Inside I reasoned, "It's my own flesh, what could be a better donor?" His surgical team completed the feat over several hours of time, cutting through and down to clean out bits and pieces of shattered bone.

Michael had driven up from San Diego for the late evening surgery. He called family in Washington and reported, "It went well. Now we wait and see if it takes." My body's intelligence took over what would be a four-year healing process. There were many stages of pain management. Muscle use adaptation and left–right side balance took years. Hatha yoga and eventually Kundalini yoga would become a saving grace.

The surgery recovery floor was my new home away from home. A burn victim's sand-filled bed eased some of the pain. I asked the nurse to pop in a Corrine Bailey Rae CD my brother had brought for me. A recently gifted Sony player sang out her lyrics to "Trouble Sleeping": *"This constant compromise, between thinking and breathing. Could it be—I'm suffering because I never give in—don't say that I'm falling in love..."* I boogied with my arms to a sweet-voiced artist I'd never heard before, as the nurse joined in smiling and later said, "You are an example for us all." I was, indeed, falling in love. Finally after years of Self-denial, I was ready to give in, to throw in the proverbial towel of thinking I'm in control of life.

A few weeks later, while being wheeled back to 5 North on a new First Step air mattress, I wondered what I would sleep on at home. Definitely pillows would be needed to rest between my bony knees. During a routine post-surgery visit Dr. Orloff commented on the rapidness of my recovery, "Much faster than normal. When he stopped in to check on healing and later remove the stitches, I offered, "We grew up Adele Davis nutrition kids. Encouraged to play sports."

"That definitely made a difference," he acknowledged.

Discharge neared. I protested when Leigh, O.T., grinned, her "ready, set, go" smile. "Time to try something new!" she exclaimed. It was not a question, but it felt like one. Toilet exercises were Leigh's 'something new'. The bedpan and bedside porta potty were safe familiar territory. Supervision from nurses was required. I felt scared and whimpered, "I can't."

Leigh guided me, step by step. One leg over the side of the bed, joined by the other. I reached out for walker handles, pushed up onto the walker, and made it over to the in-room bathroom. I felt weak and protested, "I can't do it." Lovely Leigh was unstirred, "Yes, you can." End of story.

Wasn't I the delighted fifty-one-year-old potty trainee! It was my first visit to a throne since the loss of consciousness event in late May. It was rehabilitation bliss.

Minor falls in the hospital and eventually at home were shrugged off. The joy of improving functionality ruled. Once taken for granted skills slowly returned, along with a newfound respect for daily living. And an appreciation for the benefits of practicing.

Third Life Process

Our Third Life Process relates to matters of self-esteem. How we feel about ourselves determines the quality of our lives. The open, balanced state of the third chakra determines the level of our personal power. Stage Three challenges may be the most crucial on our path and its spiritual truth and benefits the most personally fulfilling.

When we integrate this chakra's spiritual energy, we experience self-esteem, self-confidence, self-respect and empowerment. Combined they support our ambition, confident action, and the ability to take risks. We build strength of character as our self-esteem/personal power center matures. During this chakra's opening, our ethics and generosity of spirit blossom and enhance our trustworthiness.

Our third chakra wheel is located at the solar plexus, the area an inch or two above the navel. Its energy connects physically with our small intestine, gallbladder, liver, stomach and middle spine. Stage Three energy resonates with the mental-emotional energy of our personal power center, which contains the magnetic core of ego personality. Learning to be the trustworthy "lead character" in our life story is the personal challenge of this stage. Self-esteem development is its core life lesson. Learning to respect and honor our Self is its essential spiritual truth.

The sacred energy of this center matures us toward self-understanding: how do we stand on our own? Are we able to take care of ourselves? How do we balance our personal power with spiritual integrity? And how do we develop our self-esteem?

On the immediate surface, Stage Three changes relate to any and all aspects of physical self-expression. We may decide to lose weight, or change our hairstyle and way of dress to demonstrate our new self-image. We mature to embrace a self-expressed lifestyle.

Stage Three energy also relates to our physical boundaries. Beyond personal appearance, our personal strengths and weaknesses relate to Stage Three challenges and life lessons. Yet our acceptance (or critique) of our physical attributes is the simplest measure of third chakra maturation.

The Self-Esteem "Process"

Though there is a tendency to conceptualize self-esteem as a "thing" or personality quality, it actually is a process. The process of gaining self-esteem is one of the major aspects of self-development.

As maturing adults we begin having our own sense of authority, apart from group dictates, familial or societal. During this passage of the process, we grow through our individuation.

We depart from needing outer approval and authority to determine our self-worth. We learn to stand on our own two feet and take a stand for who we are becoming. Now speaking from a genuine sense of self, we can measure our conscious growth by the courageous willingness to express our authentic self. When we embark on this challenge, it may feel like a mini or major revolution. Individuating out of tribal or partnership authority is often uncomfortable.

This center's energy dynamic responds to a *healthy ability* to set ourselves apart. We cultivate this by establishing *independent* mind-emotion currency. It is our self-sufficiency energy bank. Our revolt tilts and tips the scales on our lower-stage need for attention or approval.

And so we reorganize our life choices, based on healthy ego development prompts, and become better able to take them out into the world. We learn the power of balanced personal choice. The strength of our inner life relaxes the grip of outer world's "urgent" traps, attachments, and control games.

Confidence exists, relative to our improved self-esteem. Until esteem grows, we may be oversensitive to criticism, real or imagined. Reactionary defensiveness is a sign of low self-esteem. An improved ability to respond within ourselves and with others causes us to be accountable for our thoughts words and deeds. Integrity becomes a cherished value.

The Dawn of Self-Inquiry

This leads to our next self-esteem development passage: a capacity to self-inquire. Self-inquiry is the introspective art of self-examination. We learn to ask ourselves definitive questions, such as: "Where is my allegiance focused?" and "What am I aligned with in life?"

When self-inquiry dawns, we begin deeply contemplating the illusions of "clock time." Empowered to settle into our own present-moment skins, we listen for inner cues and direction in life. We have enough self-esteem to ask introspective questions in all areas of our life. We are interested in our assessment of how well the external factors in our life serve our true needs and wants. We take responsibility for and ownership of self-respect. Any form of addictive-attachment is reevaluated as self-esteem matures. Harmful habits no longer dictate our self-respectful behavior.

Through self-inquiry, we build spiritual trust. Trust expands exponentially as we continue our inner work. Inner Support gives us courage to observe habits and patterns of thought-emotion frequencies that no longer resonate positively. We may experience inner conflict while our outer life shows signs of upheaval. These are symbolic displays of our evolving desire for change.

When we commit to change, thought-emotion patterns that create havoc, upsets and disorder are released. Through self-inquiry, we notice them and expand to choose higher perspectives encouraged by our increased self-esteem. We become empowered to select resonant beliefs.

A development of inner stamina serves us well, as we commit to ask and answer self-inquiries. This passage is our exploration, where our personal self meets our spiritual power. When we are ready for change, our growing self-knowledge supports our direction and choice of action.

Meeting Choice, Challenge and Change

With increased self esteem we learn to make choices and take actions that satisfy our newfound responsibilities in life. Self-discipline becomes accessible to us in this passage. We grow able to take personal risks while embarking actively toward responsible changes in our life.

Stage Three Life Process challenges us to *create* and *live from* our authenticity, however subtle or dramatically different our new worldly identity may appear from who we have been in the past. We may shock, surprise, or delight those close to us. We change, of our own accord, for no one but ourselves. In this stage, positive narcissism is a healthy sign of growth.

A growing certainty that *there is more to us than meets the eye* begins to rise from within. The truth that *we are not our body or the body of our life situations* begins to take root and strengthen. In early development states of this passage, we may want to introvert and "hide our inner light" under the proverbial bushel basket. This would be a sign of the Stage Three imbalance called reactive self-protection. The third Life Process is a vulnerable stage as those who know us may disagree with our individual choice to change.

Staying the course builds fortitude, which is much needed as we recreate our personal identity. That which better suits our higher perspective may help us strengthen, change, or reestablish personal boundaries. We begin to choose our company wisely in support of our growing self-esteem. The company we keep reflects our personal values.

Healthy narcissism is selfishness at its best, being in service to our spiritual grounding. Responsibility for our inner needs helps prepares us for the final passage of self-esteem development.

The Rise of Intuition

Chakra three's open and balanced energy (in unison with upper chakras) increases our intuitive listening. Respect for higher levels of intuition gains ground in our evolutionary passage of matured self-esteem and personal power. Our spiritual evolution is an inner process that commands self-esteem to do its bidding out in the world. Higher spiritual values are lived without compromise once we become advanced with this passage. Principles of spiritual dignity are upheld in outer circumstances. To the extent that outer circumstances begin to shift relative to the higher quality of our presence, we begin to notice a connection between our inner calm and life situations. Intuitive inklings we felt throughout our life begin showing us deeper meaning.

What strengthens our connection with intuition, beyond the basic instinct of lower energy centers, is an ability to be present. We become able to notice, feel, sense, and observe what thought-feeling response we have to life's events. Intuition is our perpetual ally—moment to moment—throughout our life. It offers us essential information that supports our forward movement. **Breath to breath, following our intuitive sensibility is the artful practice of a conscious life.** This richly rewarding practice guides us on our transformative path and empowers us to take trustworthy risks as we transform change and grow.

How do we strengthen our intuitive ability? With patient, present practices. Sitting, walking and moving meditation practices support daily awareness of our experiences and environments. We learn to turn within, to listen to our still, small voice, allowing intuition to guide us. This flourishing sense of autonomy gives rise to increased clarity of choice. It begins to empower us to address self-esteem issues with unflinching observation. Our Stage Three challenge is to regain our personal power in a healthful, self-accepting manner.

Our evolved sense of self, if allowed to thrive, offers us constant inner guidance. Its higher perspective will help us break the chains of self-diminishment, or lack of self-esteem, developed since birth. Our ability to make positive decisions arrives when we learn to like and trust ourselves. We rely on Internal Support to develop this muscle.

Our inner voice, when connected with our fourth chakra heart center, becomes our Inner Teacher/personal guru. Intuitive hints and clues are the whispers of our essential spiritual companion, guiding us while we grow in consciousness.

Stage Three low-self-esteem issues often express themselves within our relationships. Either we attempt to impress others or we play down our strengths to gain some form of personal security or recognition. Such behavior is based on an unconscious, misinformed belief that we are unworthy. This self-diminishing expression of lower energy may exist in our professional relationships as well. Maturing our self-esteem is crucial for all areas of our life, most especially health and well-being.

How We Cultivate Self-Worth

Self-worth is an earned quality. We want to mature our self-understanding. We learn to address early childhood fears through consciously experiencing adulthood's personal power issues. In this way, we grow beyond emotionally crippling limitations and become empowered to rely on our personal strengths.

Fear of criticism and needing to look good to feel good about our self, are signs of imbalanced third-chakra energy. Fear may limit our risk-taking skill, which requires acceptance of mistakes, or mis-steps, along the way. We may feel insecure and criticize ourselves if our outer image: appearance, profession, or education is different than societal norms. These are Stage Three energetic challenges, which pass as we cultivate self-worth.

Fear of rejection may arise when we outwardly express newfound strengths, but it does not last. Our growing self-respect does not flinch at real or imagined opinions of others.

Ironically, despite the joy we may feel having stepped into a new worldly identity we eventually discover that our self-worth has less to do with identity and more to do with being Who We TRULY Are. And being of service from this place. This sacred truth unites with upper chakras and matures us beyond self-interests with an evolved generosity of spirit.

Stage Three lessons empower us to care for ourselves from a code of ethics reflecting our strength of character. At the same time, forms of codependency dissolve as we respectfully recognize that others are capable of caring for themselves as well. We make choices based on our Heart's desires, surrendering the need to compare ourselves or our choices with others. Competitive urges fade as we respect the achievements of others and honor our self-reliance and self-sufficiency.

We willingly examine our strengths and weaknesses, not to compare or self criticize, but to know ourselves in relation to life circumstances. Empowered by our self-inquiries, we make changes wherever we recognize the need for strengthened resolve. And with kind regard for our weaker points, we acknowledge and utilize our strengths.

Our third chakra energy resonates out from the highest wheel of the material realm's lower chakras. Its sacred positioning symbolically teaches us the importance of evolving ourselves first, before we may be of benefit to others. It supports our connection with developing open and balanced Stage One and Stage Two energy with matured self-respect.

When stagnated in Stages One or Two's underdeveloped energy dynamic, we may have felt a servitude relationship with God-Source. **Third chakra energy invites us to go inside and meet a Master energy that generously serves our full awakening**. This shift begins when we turn our attention away from outer activity. Able to close our eyes, relax and look inside, where we may recognize and honor our spirit in silent readiness.

We become "still and know that I am God" inside. Source energy, in its Stage Three expanded maturity, is our little mind turning inward to meet and be with Inner Higher mind. **To be released from suffering, and delivered to the joy of being, means we discover a practice of allowance of noisy mind.** *We sit in still silence, watch our thoughts drift by from a state of pure awareness.*

Nurtured awareness reminds us that thoughts are fleeting, unreal. And that aware presence's guidance is available throughout our waking day.

If we are stuck in Stage Two control-issue energy, it reflects our refusal to accept Stage Three's spiritual antidotes. When regular visits with inner senses become our solution-seeking avenue, our overactive intellect (imbalanced sixth chakra) begins to quiet down. It is an exercise that gives us an ability to reorient our conditioned psychological responses.

We become empowered with new perceptions. Discover new perspectives of outer conditions. Our new perspectives will relieve and release the psychological angst of fear's playmates: worry and doubt, guilt and shame. These are the collective stumbling blocks when we are developing self-esteem.

The ability to "return to center" is a sacred invitation, a gift Stage Three maturation avails. Our inner refuge from personal fear and confusion is essential for the next stage's heart-opening process work. Our restful awareness practices offer us peace and solace while we complete any unfinished business that would block a fully opened Heart (fourth) chakra.

Stage Three Self-Inquiry

**Enjoy full, deep, long...Inhales...Releasing
your breath fully Exhaling...
Give yourself as many conscious breaths as you choose...**

**Take a moment to settle into a comfortable
distraction-free environment**

~ How do I feel about myself? Describe what you like: Why do I
  like this aspect of me?

~ What don't I like about me? Describe in detail:

~ What are my best attributes and strengths? What are my weaknesses?

~ What is my definition of self-respect? Do I meet my highest standard?

~ Do I respect my self-agreements? Am I able to keep my commitments to the things I want to change?

~How do I care for my personal needs?

~ Am I willing to take risks, to go beyond my present comfort zone? If not, what do I believe about myself that is holding me back?

~ Am I sensitive to the opinions of others? (Describe what comes up for you.) Am I open to reliable feedback? (Elaborate on what comes up for you.)

~Do I ever compromise my self-worth in order to be liked or loved?

~ Have I ever compromised myself in order to feel secure or have my basic needs provided for?

~ Do I seek attention or approval from others? What are my motivations?

~ Am I honest and authentic when I express myself? Do I hold back or alter the truth about personal experiences? If so, where and with whom do I communicate in this manner?

~ Do I feel guilty for my personal issues? Do I blame others for my challenges in life?

~ What do I most want to change? What steps have I taken to begin?

Here is an opportunity to go to the Micro Moves.

Self-Care Selections

We grow to love ourselves, exactly as we are. Part of that process is commitment to our self-care choices. Here are a few areas we want to develop and attend to throughout our lives. Enjoy revisits with these prompts until you have a firm foundation you honor with beneficial regularity.

Spirit Practices:

~ What is my current alignment with Divine assistance?

~ What is my current meditation and/or prayer practice?

~ How often do I connect with Higher Self?

Heart–Mind Practices:

~ What one thing am I willing to let go of today? (Helpful clue, 'thing' is any inner or outer condition that stagnates your vibrant Life.)

~ What three to five things am I grateful for today?

Body Practices:

~ How fully am I caring for my body?

~ How often do I practice conscious breathing?

~ How often do I stretch or practice yoga?

~ How often do I partake in cardio-aerobic movement?

~ How do I relate with food? Water? Alcoholic beverages? Is there anything I'd like to change about these relationships?

Self -Responsibility:

~ What would be my ideal self-nourishment practices?

~ How balanced is my self-care with my active schedule? Too little? Too much? Just right for now? What would I like to change about my self-care commitment?

~ When will I begin?

~ How will I continue and be consistent?

~ Is this something I will begin independently? Or would it be more self-responsible to ask for support?

HEART POWER

Listen

to your inner voice.

Trust your intuition,

your deep inner wisdom...

for when the time is right,

your heart will always

tell you what

you seek to

know...

CAROLINE JOY ADAMS

Fourth Inspiration

Our heart sees, feels truth. Our life situations give us opportunities. To grow True Love: the highest expression of inclusive love and forgiveness unified. Our heart respects our intrinsic sameness. Infinite Beings in mortal bodies. Interconnected Spirits in the material.

Our forms are able to sense, feel, and express great joy and deep sorrow. One child's birth or death is as moving as another's. No matter their nation, faith or family of origin. Separation is a false perception of reality. Perpetuated—used relentlessly against humanity.

We allow Life experiences to break open a hardened protective shield. Our wizened conscious choice wants return to Oneness. Courageous willingness fuels us on. We first clean up the suffering thought-emotion mess that suffocates our heart. Combined joy and sorrow alchemize into Inclusive Compassion.

Our true Nature arises from the ashes of conscious process. Our wholly, holy, whole Self, a sacred energy field, lives in us and around us. It waits for us, veiled by separation's disguises of guilt, blame and shame. Cultivated respect and reverence frees our Heart that knows our origin of Oneness.

The thirteenth century Persian poet Rumi gave us a mystic's glimpse. His ancient field beyond right-doing and wrong-doing calls to us. When we meet on the fertile ground of Truth. We realize our Self and shared connectivity. Common-unity. Community.

Psychological fear stems from conditioned ego-minds. This fear filled mind's belief in separation activates violent disputes, religious wars and more.

Once we realize Who We Truly Are, one spirit, that spirit never dies. That we are here to Live-evolve, its grip can be loosened. Our lightness of Being begins to shine. Like the original sweet Hearts we are. We remember we are Love. We are empowered to live.

True sadness is a gift. It is part and parcel of the human journey. Living through then beyond the veil of separation's sad moments deepens our love. We honor physical death, with wisdom's loving-kindness. And become harmless ourselves. In thought word and deed.

Our spirit's calls us to grow our Heart's metaphoric muscle. Energized we engage with Life compassionately. We choose inclusive love instead of fear. It is a passionate dance of JOY—as Source energy expresses Itself—as us.

We naturally love one another—once we live the truth of our unified Being. And allow grace's restoration of inclusive compassion--that Love Is.

Every Breath is Healing

In late October 2007, we neared my hospital discharge. "Every time you declined, you started back from zero," Cynthia reported to me. "Time and time again we watched you—once, twice, three times— you didn't give up." Her memory of my hospitalization process was predictive of changes yet to come.

We, that is: John, Leigh, Cynthia and I, were driven in a hospital van to visit my Burbank condo for a physical safety inspection. I felt enthused anticipation for the visit, having not seen my home for many long months. I was extremely grateful for this special pre-discharge consideration being arranged. My skilled therapist friends of the last five months gave their professional opinions to my former film-industry colleague. Tim, an expert construction coordinator, accepted their advice on what areas to "safety" in my two-story home. Staircase railings, a shower seat and bathroom bars were added in time for my upcoming return. My Shabby Chic sofa needed to be raised to a height that accommodated my limited strength, as I was unable to stand up from low-level seated positions. A film construction crew had lifted the sofa onto a wooden platform, "movie magic" style, before I returned home.

Cynthia recalled this visit. "You were very fragile. We had concerns, probably rooted in the first time we'd released you in March, back then you were readmitted a few months later.

I had expressed these same fears to my sister Regina. We had a good plan. Cynthia added, "You were going to have to be extremely brave, being single, with a family-out-of-town status. You wouldn't be able to climb those fourteen townhouse stairs for awhile. You were on your own. I remember thinking, 'she has to come *here* and learn how to live?' It looked daunting. We held our breath and hoped for the best."

I had learned a very large lesson around asking for help. My assigned St. Joseph's case manager coordinated with Kathleen Pennington, my motion picture industry case manager. Together with Regina's social work expertise, they helped prepare support systems for my next stage of rehabilitation. Regina researched outpatient therapy and nursing care companies, and then conferred with both case mangers. Dynamic Nursing, a twenty-four-hour caregiver service, and Rehab Without Walls for outpatient therapy were agreed upon. Thanks to Regina's social work background, not only did I segue into expert care and training, she'd had the foresight back in June to contact Motion Picture Industry insurance. She reported my events and hospitalization, and requested special dispensation. Motion Picture Industry insurance coverage processed her request. Months later they declared, by board vote, my case a 'catastrophic incident'. Every retroactive expense from June 2007's readmission for bi-lateral stroke through outpatient rehabilitation and nursing care would be covered.

Days before I was discharged, D'vorah knocked on my wide-open door.

I smiled as she entered. She looked quiet. Something was up. Miriam, a clinical social worker, followed as Father Mark, the Catholic chaplain I had spoken with a few times, entered alongside her. They reverently surrounded the raised railing of my hospital bed. D'vorah spoke unbelievable words: "Phillip has passed away."

Our mentally handicapped younger brother, Phillip, teacher of compassion as we grew up, had experienced a painless heart attack. It hit me like an emotional ton of bricks. I cried gut-wrenching tears.

I lost my breath. The three wise counselors held space for me to weep. Calmly they listened to my spontaneous declarations of grief. Prayers of blessings for the goodness of Phillip's life and transition were shared.

Later D'vorah, in a private moment, soothed me with her words. I'd spoken to her of Phillip's monk-like love affair with nature. "Antoinette, his freed spirit is now embraced by Nature's love. There is nothing hindering him any longer."

Phillip, born three years after me, had forceps crush his infant skull during delivery. He emerged hydrocephalic. As he grew bigger, so did his head, proportionally larger than his body. His true heart outsized them both. His sweet energy with and for nature taught us all, and teaches me still, how to be present with nature's beauty. Phillip's pure example of innocent love and sudden death at forty-eight encouraged me to get on with life. My heart broke open further. His unexpected departure, while I was in a physically fragile and emotionally vulnerable state, caused me to mourn a lifetime of losses. Thank you forever, Phillip, for blessing my heart.

Chaplain D'vorah wheeled me to the hospital chapel for a goodbye moment. She gave farewell blessings and sent me home with a precious gift: *"Every Breath is Healing"*—words written on a sturdy stripe of white cloth, given her by her rabbi. It now rests on my meditation altar, front and center, graced by images of Jesus and Buddha both in meditation pose. And other symbolic reminders of our true Nature. After prior and recent years of wounded-inner-child healing work, I reverently added my first-grade photo. Little Antoinette's soft smile now sits gold framed among my heaven on earth collection. Her healed heart feels safe and loved as we magically co-create daily. You will meet her reuniting with me in a Stage Five's Passage story "Adult Time Outs".

Recovery Without Walls

Dr. Lupo's rehabilitation follow-up notes the day before a November 2, 2007, hospital release read: "Discharge date declared: debilitation due to prolonged hospitalization."

I was ready to leave. I had gotten over my fear of returning home. Sitting outside my room in a hospital wheelchair, I met the director of Dynamic Nursing care. He introduced a few of the caregivers who would be with me 24/7. Big changes were ahead for a former Miss Independent lone wolf.

Being utterly stopped was welcomed for awhile. I understood it was exactly what was needed. I do not believe I would ever have slowed down or adopted a healthy pace, on my own. It wasn't in my pre-event mind's conditioned programming. I accepted having my ass kicked in to consciousness. The experience was embraced as a generous gift from Spirit.

Rehab Without Walls entered my home life in early November after discharge from St. Joseph's. Susie Wong, occupational therapist, Kuan Huang, physical therapist, and Ike Mendoza, clinical mastered social worker, assessed my condition and reviewed the hospital therapist's discharge notes. We slowly began eight months of rehabilitation efforts.

Team RWW became my "common-sense living" trainers. Dynamic's twenty-four-hour in-home nursing caregivers began immediately.

A physically challenged person's accoutrements were an immediate necessity. Michael delivered Shelia's (my sister-in-law) deceased dad's brand new porta potty and perfect-sized wheelchair. A sized-to-fit walker with tray and other handy items were ordered in the hospital and sent home with me. New aids for limited independent movement and safe daily living lent physical support and added a modicum of balance.

Kuan continued my physical therapy while Susie taught me practical daily occupational skills. Ike's clinical social worker instruction rounded the team's expert knowledge by supporting my social adaptation to the outer world's eventual challenges. They encouraged, taught and witnessed my return to a semblance of normal living. They patiently led the way.

During the arduous work, I remained committed, yet often pushed my mind and body too hard. It was a continuous energy-bank dance: *Stop. Go, Pause, Stop. Go to Sleep.* I had never learned healthy regulatory use of my energy allotment for each day. My outpatient therapists monitored my movement and energy depletion ceiling. Energy availability was recorded weekly, similar to the daily acute rehab reports in the hospital.

Susie imparted one of my favorite new adult living skills: "You can start over again, any time of the day, whenever you chose." Brilliant, practical advice merged with resurrected spiritual practices to assist my body's functional recovery. Another "better living" technique, never utilized prior to being stopped, was instructed by Susie. She encouraged me to use it whenever I grew tired. I still hear her, like an angel on my shoulder: "Antoinette, any task you can do as easily sitting down as standing up—sit down." I was learning self-care, self-management, as well as energy responsibility. These days—while writing—I stand up for regular breaks, breathe and stretch, able to ask myself, "What else does my body need?"

Progress made with the support of Team RWW led to being asked if I felt up to going outside. You bet! Eventually, walks around the neighborhood were suggested. Sonya, one of the Dynamic Nursing qualified C.N.A. caregivers, walked with me, counting how many blocks of energy usage felt good. Then she deftly calculated when it was a good time to turn around and go home. Following therapist-directed improvement-building exercises was much more interesting in outer-world environments. Kuan and Susie held one joint therapy session on a grassy ball field at a nearby foothill park. They asked what recreational activities or sports I enjoyed, to reengage body-brain firings with once familiar neurological instructions. Softball was my game of choice. We played with very light-weight balls. A softball player since youth, I was physically humbled at my lack of aim, arm strength, and hand-eye coordination to catch the ball into my mitt. I laughed while they encouraged. Whatever we did, I knew it was good for my overall recovery.

My appetite for day-to-day living brought with it a renewed willingness to be consciously present. The deeper meaning of life, that I was brought back to embrace, embody was showing itself.

By mid-March 2008, Ike drove me to downtown Los Angeles on a social worker contributory mission. We made jokes about him christening by name the British-accented GPS voice in his Honda SUV. I think it was called Nigel—forget exactly what he called it—but said it had a Notting Hill tonal quality. Ike assisted me with paperwork in the process of applying for a Los Angeles County Paratransit Access pass. Within a matter of weeks, I received a photo ID, unrestricted, free LA County transportation pass that expired February 2011. Team RWW encouraged me to go on MTA buses as a way of social assimilation. Eventually, I complied and practiced walking, balancing and sorting out cognitive details of bus routes.

Much later feeling adventurous, I utilized the pass on a solo excursion to historic Olivera Street via Metrorail. At this point I was still unable to drive. Michael had returned the damaged Tahoe while I was in hospital, since the leased had expired. I was driven where I needed to go for nine months.

Ike and Susie teamed up their expertise and had my Burbank YMCA membership reactivated. When I fell apart, another Michael-handled detail was to take advantage of the Y's extended-absence policy. It saved me paying for an unusable membership. I was enthused to rejoin the Y and discover what areas I could still utilize. Susie and Kuan thought pool therapy and Hatha yoga (two movement practices I'd said I liked) would be a perfect adjunct. The YMCA's inclusive policy allowed a licensed private therapist to work with his or her clients. Susie carried my inch-and-a-half-thick Everlast exercise pad. We walked into Tanya Greve's Hatha yoga class, seeking out a comfortable spot. Tanya, also a certified yoga therapist, noticed and welcomed our attendance. She was not the least bit surprised when I laid there a good amount during that first class. Nearly a year later working with Tanya in private sessions accelerated the improvement of my right-brain, left-brain balance. As of this writing, I am almost able to stand in tree pose—almost. She also anchored my new reverence for breath by training me in focused belly breathing. Lying on my back, knees raised and bent to ease tender sacral healing, I learned to inhale and feel my chest rise first. And notice as air filled my recovering lungs and feel my belly rise. Our breathwork contributed to an unprecedented recovery of total lung capacity.

Kuan, a triathlete as well as a mastered physical therapist, happily drove me for water therapy sessions in the Y pool. We began with easy movements in the shallow end of the lap pool. Eventually I water-jogged the lane with a waist float. My efforts and Kuan's know-how helped strengthen brain function as well as muscular development. In a safe, soft, watery environment, I was uninhibited. Fearless of falling, I wore props that also helped me feel safe. I played in the water like a kid just unleashed for summer break. Kuan and I laughed up a good giggle-storm often. Great for deep breathing! She and I ended up keeping in touch and going on occasional hikes.

Ike held a March meeting in my condo, with three of my adjacent unit neighbors. Ron, Bill and Marvin had been invited to help create an "In Case of Emergency" safety net.

The invitation to my three longtime neighbors read, "I am hoping my doctors and therapists agree. I want to start reducing the overnight caregiver's hours. The therapists' consensus is that I will be fine on my own one night a week, and eventually three or four. Would you volunteer and allow me to call you, if and only if I need help?" The meeting was a success. The neighbors' "I.C.E." numbers were tucked away in my cell phone, and written on a contact list as well.

Nearing the conclusion of RWW's contributions, Susie and I sat in my upstairs bedroom office alcove. I eagerly discussed my relentless desire to return to the film industry. Worried about how I would earn a living, I was thinking (too much) that my old life of familiar and known territory was my only choice. I missed the camaraderie, along with the associated ego buzz I enjoyed as a film-industry insider. I did not comprehend that I was nowhere near ready in spirit, mind and body integration to reenter the rush and swirl of the work-a-day world. And certainly not the frantic-paced profession of my prior years. The on-set invitation to not take our work deadly serious—"We're not curing cancer here" or "This is not brain surgery"—was never appreciated in my heart.

Susie had astutely recommended I give myself more time and look more closely at my concept of achievement. Ike reminded me that, no matter what I would do, I brought decades of experience and knowledge. He actually softly said, *"Remember what you bring to any situation."*

I had never seen myself in that light, before hearing and understanding the totality of what Ike said. Higher wisdom was on hold, as my new brain rebooted sufficiently to join with my heart, downloading a new program for life.

Life as I had known it shifted every day. Nothing would ever be the same. I was finally realizing this obvious truth, happy to be breathing. Yoga continued to be a major component of my inner and outer healing. At first, Kundalini yoga classes were too much, too intense and fiery. I gradually embraced their purification element as a key ingredient in my integrative healing process. Practice shined a light and eventually helped me release mental motional patterns that had smothered my heart. Honoring our chakra energy centers may someday be taught more widely. I certainly hope so.

By late May, I was able to get out to coffee with friends. Donna picked me up. She remembers our visit in her blog: "My friend is a poster woman for 'positivity'. On that day, we talked about her illness—she saw it as an incredible opportunity. She truly believes this. She said she had no idea her situation had been dire; this is something she realized over time. She didn't know I had seen her during her coma. *I did not tell her we were certain we had lost her.* She informed us that she's giving herself a birthday party, as she had missed last year's. 'Yeah I was lying unconscious on my bathroom floor,' she laughed."

Travel Matrix

Angie, a volunteer from St. Joseph's, helped me shop for a new car. Though I still wasn't ready to drive, I knew I wanted a smaller, lighter vehicle with better fuel efficiency. I picked a Toyota Matrix.

Susie, O.T had referred me to Lee Hirsch, owner and operator of Mobility Quest. Behind the wheel of Lee's double-brake and gas tank of a car, during my first time out onto the neighborhood streets, I was a bit nervous and scared—again. We trained together for a month or so before driving on a freeway onramp, then right back off again. Yikes! Lee recommended that I start driving my new Matrix around familiar streets. Driving took time to get used to. I love mobility and travel, so it was a big part of the independence I wanted to regain. The smaller Matrix mirrored an exponential shift in my changing values. Conscious downsizing felt good.

On June 1, 2008, I celebrated my birthday with friends and neighbors. Two cakes were decorated with festive candles, one for 2007 side-by-side with 2008.

As my self-trust deepened, I accepted a wedding invitation for Jennifer Dunne's Fourth of July weekend celebration nuptials. She and Justin Rowland had selected a lakeside lodge on Sandpoint Idaho's Lake Pend Oreille. I took my first plane trip since returning, unwell, from Mexico in 2006. The sky was lit up by fireworks and love that Fourth of July evening.

The Idaho trip was a test drive for a much-hoped-for trip to Mexico. Where I wanted to see and thank my circle of friends in the Yucatan Peninsula. Their prayer energy had kept me going on more levels then one. Lucy Flores had watched over my little foreign property. She and husband Luis's family had prayed for me as well. Anuar Santiago and Waldo Perez, two of my best friends on the planet, met me at Cancun International Airport in late July. The e-mail I'd sent to friends and practitioners requesting comments for this book received this reply from Anuar: *"Dear Antonieta, The saddest time in our friendship was when I saw you arrive in Playa with your cane. I hid my tears. You are a warrior. You are back on the path meant for you. Remember, things happen and sometimes we don't understand why—in the moment. But in the end, you know there was no other option to change your life path. We love you and wish you the best."* Truth simply put, amigo mio.

Simplifying was part of my life-changing process. Kathleen Pennington, my Motion Picture Case manager, also a former nurse, had graced me with a home visit back in mid-winter 2008. "I see you someday living in a ground-level dwelling." Ironically when I bought the Burbank foothills condo in 1991, that had been my exact plan. Own it for a while, then sell it and move into a small house. Eighteen years later and near death events reconnected me with my original vision. I was willing to dream again and celebrate life.

Unseen Forces

There I was, alone, able to sit on my living room's platform raised sofa in silence. The therapists and nurses were gone. It was time to deepen my connection with Source, to make friends with the Invisible, to leave more of the known and familiar behind.

I had talked about, read about, attended seminars on self-realization. I'd participated in consciousness retreats and workshops. I had not walked my talk. My intellect (unlike our true Intelligence) had grasped at outer-world trappings and deflected the thriving spaciousness of Source for years. My truest self had waited. I understand now what was missing in all my previous efforts. An eternally present Inner Teacher had been with me all along. Teacher's presence, an intuitive whisper, is a sense-ability that had grown stronger with recent outer events. My deeper listening had improved as my hamster-on-a-wheel dysfunctional relationship with time neared its end. The gift of patient, present practice had birthed out of the focus needed to learn everything again.

Carmen had given me a meditation consultation at my fifty-second birthday celebration. I drove my 2009 Matrix to Pause Your Mind in Venice, California. Linda from the ICU story sat with me in her womb-like meditation center. She concluded our two-hour session with two simple words: "Be it." We had talked about what I felt happening inside me. Her guidance helped my evolving spiritual maturation, numerous times. Once we know Who We Are and honor the truth of our Beingness, there is no-thing left to do—just be, and all else follows.

Intuition guided a trip to Northern California. A solitary, weeklong woodsy retreat would further clear my mind. It was a return to our Earth Mother's healing powers. While I watched yearlings munch for nourishment outside my Harbin Hot Springs bathroom window, an insight occurred. I walked out the door of the monkish accommodations. There sat an elderly woman on the rustic bench between our balconied rooms. Our pine-tree-graced conversation ended with smiles. My mind was clear. I'd heard and felt my next step. It was time to leave the past behind. Sell the condo. Many more lifestyle changes were ahead.

I returned to Burbank and watched for hints and clues that led me to a real estate broker. The condo showed and showed and showed. The market was very weak. I waited patiently in my car under Wildwood Canyon's shady trees while the realtor held open houses. I read and wrote while potential buyers walked through my home of 18 years.

My Inner Teacher sent signs and signals that my former life's doings were at an end. It softly tapped my heart: *"Your profession has changed, dear one, and you don't know it yet—there's no going back. It would not be healthy for you."* The urge to return to the film industry lingered, while it died a slow death. This sticky stubborn streak, with its dark and light sides, finally began to relax.

After a Fall 2008 monthly check up chat with Dr. Taback, I walked across Alameda Avenue and entered St. Joseph's main lobby. He agreed that I had something to offer from my ongoing recovery experiences. Cynthia was shocked and pleased as I exited 5 North's elevator. I wanted to volunteer. I returned after completing the required training and offered my listening and refreshment-cart items to 5 North acute rehabilitation patients. Here's what Cynthia remembers of my months on her staff: "Your visits on the floor, especially when you volunteered, were so important to the staff and patients. To see someone recover like you did, keeps us going. The staff felt totally acknowledged for their efforts and contributions. Patients were given hope for their own recoveries."

Once while I was volunteering, Lisa Armstrong, head of stroke recovery rehabilitation programs, was at the 5 North elevator doors. We were introduced. She graciously received my request to tour ICU. She showed me where I'd lain for months. I was floored. I had no idea what my family and friends had sat through.

I e-mailed everyone. "NOW I get it…PRETTY ominous…you are all amazing for not giving up on me."

Regina wrote back, "You and an abundance of unseen forces surrounded us. Throughout the entire time, it kept amazing us all. Causing us to stick with you---because you were signaling a fight to stay."

There had been no advanced directive in place. My family did not know how long to keep me alive. It was a challenging chain of events they watched.

Regina had followed her intuition. It led her to Chaplain D'Vorah's office. "She wants to live" was D'vorah's response. "She told me as much when I met her," she added. D'vorah's hospital notes recorded that during our July Fourth visit, though I was depressed, my word for faith was trust.

It is trust I lived within those moments onward. I learned to lessen judgment and expectation, trusting that unscheduled events are a form of spirit's guidance. It reignited a courageous willingness to change what was mine to change. I went on to co-facilitate a wellness support group with Cynthia and resume a public speaking aspiration, offering my story as inspiration to others.

During Cynthia's interview, she added, "I used you as a role model after you'd completed volunteer work, an example for stroke and wellness groups of willingness to change—using water therapy to help you learn to walk again and simplifying your life in order to change gracefully."

Those simplifications happened over time as Inner Teacher gently guided me on.

Fourth Life Process

Our entire spirit-mind-body eco-system is powered by fourth-chakra energy. Its physical mid-point is significant. Fourth-chakra sacred energy intermediates between body and spirit. This Masterful Bridge of energy mediates between our lower, physical, external-world chakras and upper, spirit-related ones. When allowed to flow freely, it is our divine emotional prosperity.

Stage Four energy—emotional energy—is paramount to our spiritual-emotional development. The lesson it teaches us develops our ability to live from the energy of inclusive love. We emanate love and compassion, once we have successfully met the life challenges this center represents. Our consciousness expands through embodiment of this stage's sacred truth: Love is the absolute and ultimate power. It governs all visible and invisible forces of life.

The fourth chakra is medially located at the heart, our chest center. It connects energetically with our heart, circulatory system, lungs, ribs, diaphragm and thymus gland. It governs energy flow through our shoulders, arms and hands.

Its mind-emotion connection relates to our emotional perceptions. Who we are being, in relation with our heart's openness, is reflected in this chakra's balanced or imbalance energy. Our challenge as adults is to move beyond misconceived childhood perceptions of love. Our conditioned responses to living from fear, instead of love, are seen as coping mechanisms that no longer serve us.

Early human development encompasses a wide range of what love is, from healthy to dysfunctional: love as compassion, hope or despair, envy or even hate. Our Stage Four challenge is to free ourselves of harmful conditioning of habitual, mental-emotional viewpoints absorbed in familial or societal environments. We mature to generate, from within ourselves, a nature of all-inclusive love—a.k.a. conscious compassion.

Our life challenge in this stage is opening to an expanded perception of life—fully embracing the universal truth that all that *was, is, or will be* is unfolding according to a Divine plan. At this stage, we become capable of trust in Source's loving intent for the evolution of our consciousness. This stage's heaven-on-earth unification invitation empowers us to "let go, let God." It calls us to be one with the power of Divine Love, to allow Source to elevate us to further levels of higher consciousness.

Our fourth stage of openness bears a resemblance to third-chakra energy development. It expands through a process of passages. At our heart center, we must learn to upgrade our self-esteem beyond Stage Three's relative level of self-esteem in relation to others and the outside world. The fourth chakra calls us to maturely honor ourselves, within every aspect of our human totality. Spirit-mind-body integration toward Wholeness is our highest earthly direction. This center's energy of unconditional love guides us there.

Stage Four energy challenges also bear a small resemblance to those of Stage Three. In the latter, we are challenged to examine our thoughts and feelings about ourselves in relation with the outer world. Fourth-chakra energy invites our focus to turn inside. We visit with the thoughts and feelings we have for ourselves. At this higher level, essential mind-emotion process work is needed to form healthy relationships, in all areas of our life.

The sacred truth that *until one loves oneself, one is incapable of loving another* describes this stage's life challenges and spiritual truth. It signifies that our fundamental mission in life is to realize personal-spiritual unification. We want a love-filled marriage between our personal self and our soulful Heart.

No matter our IQ or active mental energy, neuroscience and spiritual teachings agree, our core energy power *is* the quality of the emotions our thoughts generate. Superior to cerebral intellect, unconditional love is the purest form of Intelligence. It is One with Infinite Intelligence, an energy that pours through our entire being. We are preordained to learn and express the universal language of love.

Higher-energy frequencies of all-inclusive love and pardoning are ours to learn. How to be compassionately for-giving requires that we accept our spiritual legacy, our birthright. Placing our heads below our hearts while in yoga practices reflects an ancient sacred honoring of the power that rests within.

We are not born speaking the language of all-inclusive love or compassion. Our life's journey is composed of lessons. When they are met with our higher consciousness, we demonstrate love's pure power. How we are with the power of love determines the quality of our lives.

Our Evolving Experience of Love

Our definitions of love often follow our spiraling progression through the chakra-stages. Stage One love within the tribe may be conditional or unconditional and hold us to a necessary familial loyalty. Second-chakra love is directed outside ourselves toward others, and may contain behaviors and expressions of love we learned in childhood and young adulthood. We have learned to care beyond our blood lines. As we mature and begin nurturing ourselves, Stage Three's energy revolves around what we personally love about external aspects of life. We form our own preferences apart from family, friends or professional influences.

In the lower-chakra stages, love exists in relation to external factors. At Stage Four's sacred midpoint, we grow to learn the art of loving ourselves unconditionally. Become emotionally matured to authentically offer love to others. Contemporary psychology acknowledges that our highest feeling frequency of love has supreme influence over outcomes in our life. Finding our way back to Source energy, which creates magnificent outcomes, is this center's invitation. Love has the power to guide us on, as we process fourth chakra lessons and challenges.

Cultivating the Love that Heals Our Inner Child

Stage Four invites, our reliance on others for love and approval to shift. This chakra places full responsibility for both *completely* in our hands. Love and self-approval come with a willingness to listen to all of our feelings. Our history, from infancy to adulthood, comes with invisible, yet palpable material that blocks access to our heart power. We have, within our psyche, emotional wounds. Our heart retrieval is the most courageous act of self love we will ever embark upon.

It is a process we initiated in Stage Three's self-introspection steps. We looked closely at our perceptions, likes and dislikes of our outer life. Forth-chakra energy calls us to turn inside with willingness to find and claim our deeper truths. Our heart's messages are requests for our inward attention. Self-love demonstrates in our ability to hear and express our truths and our true feelings.

If we have unsettled childhood issues that continue to weigh us down, this absence of freedom will color every choice we make. Our essential core work is healing our wounded inner child. Until this revitalizing, yet formidable process is undertaken, any negative self-image adopted since birth dominates our psyche and continues to disrupt positive emotional energy flow.

Prior to this stage's development, we were living from a reactionary "wounded child" maturity level. We had been participating in life with its limited emotional outlook. Arrested emotional development is not uncommon for adults of all ages. Many live with partners, and in some cases they are raising children of their own, yet are still expressing from unconscious wounds that exist as aspects of dysfunctional ego.

Self-love is a spiritual act of reclaiming our inner child, whose essence will always be within us. This includes the practice of re-parenting ourselves with an open heart. We become empowered to let go of wounded-heart and wounded-mind self-images and attitudes.

Recreating our relationship with our inner child becomes delightful play once they feel our newfound sense of authority for our safety and security.

This delicate work begins with uncovering negative habitual patterns that limit our connectivity with Source, ourselves and others. We may decide we want professional counseling and support to begin this work. Some choose to independently undertake this necessary journey with assistance from self-development study and use of books equal to John Bradshaw's *Homecoming: Reclaiming and Championing Your Inner Child*.

Once we process this essential inner work, whichever self-loving method we chose, we reconnect with our original Self, our true Nature. We reclaim the gifts we came to earth to share. Our healed, re-parented inner child contains the loving and lovable energy of our best aspects gone awry.

Making the Shift from Self-Parenting to Self-Care

Fourth-chakra inner work calls us forth to examine our deepest thoughts and feelings about ourselves. Growth in unconditional self-love is our intention that involves courageous introspection. We commit to discover our thought-emotion responses, and we examine what we think and feel about ourselves. Beliefs, ideas, concepts, ambitions and attitudes are all subjects of our heart-mind's review. In this process, we tune in to the expanded or contracted state of our heart center.

During this stage, we also learn to adopt a gentle disposition of self-care. Much care is given to our emotional body's needs. Healthy choices for food, drink and companionship help support our healing self-love endeavors. It is an excavation process of deep, hidden behavior patterns that have kept us stuck in our lives, patterns that once stopped us from moving forward. And living as our greatest Self.

Their release is a courageous act that most likely will feel akin to a great loss. It is natural to cry and mourn as this death/rebirth process unfolds. The false self is dying—giving birth to authentic Self. Healing our wounded inner child is our loving heart's recovery process. The fourth chakra opens exponentially as we commit to our process and remember who we are.

Our participation with inappropriate or self-destructive relationships— be they personal or professional, is up for examination. We may have been subject to emotional or physical violence that demeaned our precious human spirit and left us feeling powerless. Therapeutic aid may be necessary to healthfully delve into extremely painful past experiences. Seeking out appropriate support, when needed, is always a healthy self-respecting choice.

Healing inner-child and adult wounds is the most worthy, necessary transformational work we do in our lifetime. The intrinsic gifts we have for the world lay beneath the sad, sorry negative self-image disguise. It is our finest recovery work, at times requiring fierce love and refined spiritual warrior energy.

Essential Lessons in Forgiveness

An essential aspect of this freeing work is lessons in forgiveness. Released from the stronghold of old wounds, we no longer think like a wounded child. We return matured, able to learn the true meaning of forgiveness. We learn how to release the past from a sacred heart-mind perception. *Forgive them (or self)—they know not what they do*, expresses mastered fourth chakra energy. In contemporary terms, we or they would have done better if we/they only knew how.

It is a loving choice when we learn to perceive all people as spirits in the material doing the best they can from their current level of consciousness. Being *for-giving* is an expression of unconditional love. Two sides of a divine coin, unconditional pardon and unconditional love constitute our priceless currency of life. As we grow in self-love, we realize that the energy of holding grievances invariably hurts only ourselves.

Once we recognize this sacred truth, we offer forgiveness gracefully. Recognizing each moment of life is a gift, we no longer want to squander our energy on petty regrets, extreme disappointments or betrayal. We connect with a steady stream of inner love and it empowers our life breath to breath. It is our inner wisdom that teaches us this: *forgiveness is greater than the belief that what was done, or what we did, was acceptable.* We mature spiritually to practice moment-to-moment forgiveness of ourselves and all others.

The wisdom of our heart teaches us that letting go is for our benefit. The cleaned, cleared magnetic power of our feeling center draws unto us all that we truly love. This is the magnificent benefit of our courageous heart-opening work. We continue on and enjoy life with conscious renewal practices of self-introspection and release.

Heart Empowerment

Once we are released from protective mechanisms, new definitions of what is truly important to us become clear. We accept the task of reviewing new ideas and concepts from our heart energy's perspective.

We willingly ask ourselves introspective questions, unafraid of what we will hear. When we ask our heart what it truly and deeply desires for us, it sparks a spirited conversation of the utmost importance to how we go forward in our lives. We listen attentively for our next, best intuitive step.

We become inquisitive we explore matters pertaining to our life circumstances and relationships from a spiritual perspective. We ask ourselves whether we are ready and emotionally available to be with people, places and things, and we no longer compromise our heart's true aspirations. We also discover what we like, what we love, and what makes us feel joyfully balanced in life. We become empowered by self-love to reexamine our strengths and weaknesses from an internal heartfelt perspective.

This stage's opening marks our return to the truth that union within oneself is essential to authentic, intimate partnership. It colors our relationships with everyone and everything in our life. Whatever support system was needed to travel through intense passages of healing-inner-child and learned-forgiveness work will be gently released. We return to the power of our heart, letting go a wounded-victim identity.

With compassion inside, we honor any lingering suffering in us while inviting heart power back into our lives. Our self-talk changes when we are anchored with love. We may uncover that it is not easy to dis-identify with wound mentality. In some situations, it keeps one tied to the familiar past. If this is the case, it is advisable to seek therapeutic assistance in order to move on.

Heart-empowered, we are able to see the hidden lessons that painful situations were meant to teach us. We recognize and accept them as our spiritual classroom's gifts. Regarding our ability to accept and appreciate all that transpired: we might simply "fake it until we make it." Appreciation for life's lessons nurtures our ability to master the conscious art of forgiveness. Being grateful for every experience that comes our way is wizened awareness.

The healthy partnership between our psyche and soulful spirit helps release any lingering victim identity from our self-image. We let go the victim persona's need for revenge or retribution wanting to respect our heart-energy flow. *A Course in Miracles* describes miracles as a change of perspective. The ability to see life through the eyes of inclusive love is the everyday miracle of a conscious mind.

Within this stage, Stage Three's learned self-esteem grows into self-respect and self-acceptance. Our heart energy center empowers self-accepted higher levels of intuition. Our first-level mindful-awareness in lower stages expands into our internal second sight (intuition) as our heart chakra opens. We notice, sense and hear deeper truths while watching and following the intuitive hints and clues that appear in daily life. Practicing allowance of renewed conscious connection with Higher Mind, we are now able to bypass gut-level instinctual reasoning, in preference for intuitive guidance.

With attention to our mindful-awareness practices, we grow in trust of intuitive messages and feel content with spending time alone. In meditative, vertical quiet, our sacred feminine (yin) energy flourishes. Intuition guides our capable horizontal masculine (yang) energy as we engage with the world. We are empowered to follow Divine guidance received with our open authentic heart.

"Things happen for a reason" becomes a respected as heart truth, while (sixth chakra) insightful awareness of the synchronicity of life events increases. A dance between calm detachment and engaged disposition is reflected in our choice-making. We become able to discern when action or non-action is appropriate, dependent upon which *feels like* the loving choice. Fear of mis-steps weakens as this center's energy awakens. We are aware that so-called mistakes are simply and invitation to renew our intentions. We allow for discovery of a next best step.

As we strengthen our inner connection with Heart Power (Divine energy), we recognize our primary relationship is with Source. Our loving respect for Self, and Inclusive love of Life has led us to the power of Creation. Less-than-beneficial external world support structures tend to melt away—be relinquished—as we realize power's true source.

The price for redeeming ourselves is learning to remain committed and gently vigilant. We breathe, relax and stay present to our thought-emotion transmissions. The power of Stage Four's openness helps us wake up to each new day, alive to the awareness of our True Nature. We're committed to remain attentive as our Heart Power expands.

Our realization that our pure heart never did the unforgivable is realized by grace of Higher Authority, and we are guided to higher perspectives. Our evolving connectivity with Source invites us to be fifth chakra empowered Co-creators, living breath to breath, being the truest expression of our Self. Trust in our intuition and inclusively-loving Self guides us on.

As a culmination of Stage Four, we have opened to perceive our life as an evolutionary classroom. Our heart is reclaimed as our ever-present Inner Teacher. We begin to embrace each day anew. Empowered, we look at ourselves in the mirror and declare the day our own. We proclaim with focused eyes of love:

Today is my day. Everything I bring to myself
is for my highest evolution and growth.

Fourth Self-Inquiry

Enjoy some full, deep, long...Inhales...
Releasing your breath...Exhaling fully...
Give yourself as many conscious breaths as you choose...

Take a moment to settle into a
comfortable environment of choice

~ How loving am I of myself? Am I easily able to look into my
eyes and express unconditional love? Am I willing to make this a
regular practice?

~ What challenging questions have I resisted asking myself? What frightens me about these?

~ What might shift in my relationship with myself with deepened self-inquiry? What may change in relationship with others?

~ Am I ever critical and judgmental? How does this behavior affect my relationships?

~ Am I holding anger and resentment? Whom, including myself, have I not forgiven in my life?

~ What is my current interpretation of forgiveness? What is its origin? How does it keep me tied to past experiences?

~ Am I willing to contemplate forgiveness as access to the power of unconditional love?

~ What would I gain by truly forgiving the past?

~ What fears stop me from moving beyond my emotional wounds?

~ Whose forgiveness would I seek to release myself of past transgressions?

~ If I am no longer in communication with this person, am I willing to write them a descriptive letter of apology, asking for their forgiveness? A message that empowers my act of contrition and self-forgiveness though it may never be sent?

~ What do I most want to express in order to ignite forgiveness of myself for past behaviors?

~ What control issues do I have? How do I interact with others in controlling manners?

~ What is my ideal description of a healthy, intimate relationship? What does intimacy mean to me?

~ Am I open to experience unconditional love in my relationships?

A Loving reminder to revisit Self-Care Selection's Heart-Mind Practices. As well as visiting Micro Moves' prompts. Enjoy your Life!

YIELD TO...WHAT IS...

Concerning all acts of initiative,
There is one elementary truth the ignorance of which kills
countless ideas and splendid plans:

That moment one definitely commits
Oneself, then Providence moves too.

Whatever you can do, or dream you can...Begin it!
Boldness has genius, power and magic in it.

Begin it now.

GOETHE

Fifth Inspiration

Hear the incessant chatter? It's in all our minds. Relax, dear ones: we think—it's human. The upside is we *are* in charge. Mental munching 'gremlin-saboteur' voice does not have to run/ruin our lives.

Our attention is a pre-requisite for positive change. We pay attention, intentionally. When we stick with it, we notice the stream of dialog that is not us. Listen to its diatribe *about* our life. Observing it is doing our life's work. Our practice of reclaiming true essence: Presence.

We honor our life with our loving attention. Our witnessing eventually slows down—even quiets the internal narratives. And engages our relatedness with All-That-Is.

We are able to witness inner and outer life—anew. We see clues in our daily living. We become capable of loving exchanges with our Self. The inner outer climate changes, for longer periods of the day, as we become the neutral watcher.

Our *devotion to being Presence* energizes our ability to co-create. We are becoming conscious *cause in the matter* of our life. Capable of co-creating new life circumstances.

Sweet soul voice offered me this: *"If it doesn't feel good, it's not me. Return to me… I will help you intuit. Will lift you up…enjoy the simplicity*

I offer...." Grew my "pay attention, dim the noise" muscle. I like feeling good. I enjoy feeling empowered to notice good-God details everywhere from the inside out.

Imagine we've learned the art of listening—observing Life anew.

Let's pretend that we're living spontaneously, moment to moment. Wondrous colors and details of life are showing themselves. We feel the peaceful thrill of watching life as it was truly unseen before. Insects, birds, plants and microcosmic nature captivate our attention. The inclination to watch raindrops and breezes in a meditative state arises. Sunrise bursts, and sunset twilights delight us.

We're seeing everything. Being with everything in us and around us.

Birds fly beneath giant oak limbs and land perched on a speed limit sign. Reminding us— mirroring our ability to pause and slow down. To glance here and glance there, before moving on. Every mini-moment of life teaches us to remember.

Earth is our green-cement-asphalt-terra firma classroom. It serves as our daily teacher while our timeless Inner wisdom listens.

We want to learn remember master the ability to enjoy Life. Relishing all of its unknowable twist and turns. Allowing it to re-mind us. As we allow our mind to surrender-yield to *what is*. We begin to notice deeper meanings. Simple clear messages appear.

A while ago, I heard rumblings of inner dissonance. I'd asked my Heart for clues. Then a MTA bus billboard flashed by with a message. I read the foot-high words, stopped at a red light: *Your future has been adjusted'.*" I had to smile, remembering All-That-Is is ultimately in charge. A mobile ad for a popular film reminded me to surrender. Heavenly details exist everywhere.

My active imagination sometimes gets carried away. I named it "clever" gremlin. Conscious discernment is a key to noticing when *heartfelt* realization pops in. I listen to *it* and follow *that* yellow brick road.

Written signals, large or small, appear often. On another dull disposition day, while driving to errands I wondered what was next. I wanted to understand and move on. The bank drive-thru granted direction. Waiting my turn, I looked straight ahead and read telling words on the bumper of a car in front of me: *"I want what I want when I want it."* I belly-laughed out loud and clapped my hands in appreciative thanks for the rightness I felt inside. As I drove forward, I felt infinitely lighter as energy poured in. Laughter's endorphin burst aided my return to sanity.

We remember. We forget. We release self-judgment. Non-resistance to whatever illusive trap our monkey-mind stirs up is a must. We surrender to witnessing our thoughts words and deeds.

Only our Presence opens our true heart's power. Which will lead us to embodiment of Unity's freedom.

Patience leads to practice. Practice leads to peaceful trust in our co-creative ability—unlike any we have previously known.

Trust Choice

In Spring 2009, meditative practices and metaphoric dream guidance offered new perspectives. One "end of the world" dream hinted at an important release from the fear of bodily death. As a dark-skied surreal Earth environment trembled, strange structures collapsed while people scurried from the cataclysmic deluge. The truth of our divine immortality left me feeling calm and gentle. Others joined me as we safe havens appeared before us. We gathered, offering solace to crying children. I woke peaceful and intrigued with the dream's messages.

Over the months, Inner Teacher whispers of what was next caught my attention. I listened closely for direction. My new profession would have something to do with what brought me back to life. And it would hinge on my ability to communicate it to others. I felt a surge, an invitation to be part of a global movement. I'd co-collaborate within a healing arts community. I had no idea where this inspiration would lead. I just felt its rightness.

Financial benefits that would fund this direction awaited my retrieval. I had not been paying attention. Retroactive monies and more had been available for months. Receptive allowance was a brand new quality for me. I had been an (over) active doer, thinking I had to make things happen. I'd lived from a left-brain dominant perspective for too long, blocking out potentials of softer, allowing Sacred feminine energy. This aha moment opened my sense of wonder. Recognition of lifelong study came alive. Creative principles I had read about were demonstrating themselves, as I learned to listen- take the right next step- then let go. I wanted to befriend "Let go, let God" and Law of Attraction principles. I wanted to get out of the way. A continuum of intentional "let go's" were in the works.

I researched a number of transpersonal psychology and coaches' training programs. An enduring passion to immerse myself in a mastery of personal growth and transformation teachings beckoned. I contacted the Coaches Training Institute based in San Raphael, California, whose international programs resonated deeply.

A half-hour sample session with Janaki Bakshi, CPCC, found me in tears. She was brilliant. She touched the nerve that needed to be touched. It was the original "self love" guidance from Louise L. Hay's *You Can Heal Your Life*. Janaki called me beautiful and strong. I cried and cried and cried. Linda had said, "Be it." These wise women knew where I stood. Their wisdom walking would inspire my own. It would be several months before I registered for CTI's next Los Angeles training program.

While my brain continued to heal, its new operating system downloaded. Meditation, yoga and conscious breath work assisted in the right-left brain dance—the being-doing balancing waltz I had been mis-stepping most of my life. Yoga therapy sessions with Tanya continued to aid this breath centered balancing process.

Healing bodywork with Carmen addressed physical aches and pains, which were slowly mending. The sacral reconstructive surgery outer scars had healed. Tender to the touch, the inner scars were still uncomfortably in process. Deep breathing and her expert intuition helped smooth out reconnecting internal tissues.

I hadn't known that Carmen administered healing touch while I was in coma. She'd sent creative healing to my Ayurvedic (marma) energy plates, later describing them to me as points along human's meridian centers. Carmen had felt for skin warmth, testing to see if centers needing additional life force. She gave her vital energy to areas of energetic dormancy.

I am eternally grateful for allowance of an outside practitioner-friend's contributions to my recovery outcome. I remember several times she came to visit with Paulin, her artist husband, while I laid in Acute Rehab. She practiced reflexology on my recovering, stroke-affected feet. I have privately joked about "my right foot" as a reminder of my good and blessed life. Its slightly clubbed toes are friendly evidence of Higher Self's guidance to come back and co-operate with continued healing work.

A Pause Your Mind weekend retreat at Santa Barbara foothill's Casa Maria created an opportunity to give thanks. Invited by Linda and Carmen, I met the circle of souls who had prayed for my life. What a joy to see their generous spirits in person and weep appreciatively in their presence.

On the final evening after our gatherings, I knocked on Linda's second floor door. She had graciously exchanged her ground-floor room when I registered at the front desk. Climbing stairs multiple times a day was not yet possible. Tired after several beautiful days in interactive sessions, I confessed to my overdoing it. I informed her that I might not make it to early morning silent meditation or the final morning's yoga gathering led by Carmen. Inner and outer healing followed its own timetable as I continued learning to listen and honor its unfolding.

By the late summer, nearly a year had passed with the real estate listing. It was time to consider a new broker. I sat at my large, glass dining room table with several. Brad Korb, well known for his positive marketing and business approach, became the trusted choice, as the condo showed I was being trained in CTI's co-active coaching model. Our five-month training was held at the LAX Marriott, at which I stayed one three-day weekend a month to honor balancing my well-being. Participating with like-hearted colleagues and mastered co-leaders was my first experimental step toward fulfilling spring's insightful vision.

Brad called in October and quietly asked, "Ready to move?" I sure was. I voluntarily collapsed a financial house of cards. An eighteen-year ownership of the condo and a twenty-five-year career ended. I was set free as they fell. I had never felt lighter in my life. The condo paid off years of credit card debt and the new Matrix as well. I no longer owed banks and they no longer owned me.

Trust in process bloomed. I opened up to change, on every level of life. Preparations for the move began. Cleared clutter of material belongings was immensely freeing. Any duplicated appliance or whatnot was given away. I shredded twenty-odd years of film industry and financial records. A Craigslist advertisement brought happy buyers of oversized furnishing I no longer needed. I was purposefully downsizing. Flat Rate Mover's truckload was streamlined once I completed extensive clearing.

Maria Keohan, a dear friend and sister, was my "move buddy" on November 13, 2009. At the end the day, while movers unpacked the house, I went to my new bedroom and closed its 1939 glass doorknob. I lay on my just-made bed, keeping a scheduled phone session with Janaki. She had since become my coach as I progressed through CTI's curriculum. I had done too much in the weeks before the move. I was wiped out. She intuitively heard it.

"What's going on?" she invited me to open up.

I wept from exhaustion. Janaki acknowledged me for keeping our appointment and challenged me as well. "I want you to consider walking away from everything around you, for the entire weekend. Let go, leave it alone. How does that sound?"

It sounded like the very thing I had never learned. Dance with balance, voluntarily. Akin to Linda and her offering, Janaki gave me two simple words. "So what" became a new useful mantra. It taught me to practice self-respect and self-nurturing when I needed them the most. I learned to wait or walk away from unessential tasks.

So what offered me a discerning wisdom of choice.

Wisdom allowed a co-creative process, full of practical, mystical magic. Life became easier to live. Helpful signs and signals became the norm. I watched and listened. Several months earlier, before the move, I had been slowly driving up and down Burbank foothills' residential streets. I knew where I most wanted to live and utilized my location-scouting skills to search for a new home. Trotta Realty's "For Lease" sign had been planted in a well-groomed lawn. It motivated me to pull to the curb for a closer look. A hummingbird seeking nectar from birds of paradise that graced a 1939 Spanish bungalow's picture windows charmed me. Its vast backyard flourished with fruitful orange and fig trees, prompting me to call the number on the sign. I would eventually watch sunrises from its bedroom window and glowing twilights through the dinette's framed windowpanes. I grew stronger and healthier each day. I watched hummingbirds glisten, their wings caressing the air in rapid figure eights. They naturally knew when to rest. And be still. Earth Mother's strength surrounded this place of recovery and soulful change. I needed a sweet, safe place for what was ahead.

Viola's Funeral

In late autumn 2009, family and friends visited. We warmed my new abode. D'vorah walked with me room to room blessing the house. New and former neighbors came over. Many dear friends stopped in with smiles and snacks.

I began intuitive co-active coaching with a few in-person clients while completing CTI training. We worked with whatever their current situations reflected. I held space as they looked inside at dark scary places and explored. Tears and laughter filled my cavernous, Spanish-style living room.

Sessions with Janaki deepened a realization. A silent violence had dominated my thought-emotion programming. I felt its shadowy contrast to the emerging softness of receptive allowance and co-creativity.

December began what I now call my 0:Dark:00 (any hour prior to sunrise) practices. I rose at 4 a.m. Silence and darkness surrounded me. No light was turned on. I dressed in the dark, purposefully blind as a "make friends with the unknown" practice. It trained me to let go and trust intuitive steps. To surrender to inner guidance, allow my soul to lead. Guide me to the next micro-movement while in the dark.

Walking in silent, empty streets, lights would begin to glow. I enjoyed meditative wandering. An occasional coyote, possum or scavenger skunk shared the moment. Unbeknownst to me, I was on the verge of a dark night of the soul. I listened and obeyed. With creativity beckoning, I wanted to clear mental clutter, remain open receptive, and dim down the static of mind-noise.

I created a Winter Solstice purging ceremony. Held in the tree-filled backyard, I read the following words. I stood on the orange tree's fertile earth, beneath the canopy of her branches.

Viola's Funeral Ceremony, December 21, 2009

Dear Viola, a.k.a. Violence,

Please accept my gratitude for all your hard efforts to protect and provide for me. I understand a fierce dysfunctional love/hate was embedded in your reactivity. I forgive you from the depth of my Heart for the cruel and twisted extreme you went to get my attention. I resign as collaborator. I forgive us both. This is goodbye. Your services are no longer needed.

Before we part, I want you to know how deeply grateful I am for the lessons you have given/shown me. You led me to my Heart's wisdom.

I give these viola seeds to our Mother Earth as an act of self-forgiveness. I bless them with words of gratitude for being awakened.

It's been a long journey. You must be tired. Rest, dear one. Rest in peace. Amen.

Blessing: "These seeds germinate, flourish and thrive. The colorful flowers that spring up from this fertile ground represent my Love and Rebirth. These heart-shaped beauties are an ancient (Greek) symbol of fertility and love. They also offer healing and sweetening gifts when utilized wisely.

Breathe. Stillness. Silence.

I burned a lengthy list of dysfunctional behavior patterns I had recognized. Ashes were given to the ground beneath a large sturdy pine. Spring of 2010 hints of green and purple flowers emerged from fertile soil of the budding orange tree.

A psychological surgery was well underway. Old habits died hard as I worked at building a coaching practice. I forced myself to continue, thinking I knew the plan. Even while I felt my uncertainty.

I needed and wanted inner help. Pre-dawn meditative walks and sitting meditations continued. I saw a few clients once or twice a week. The work was rewarding, but something wasn't as fulfilling as I had hoped. Sweet and gentle nudges were heard: *Find classic rendering of Catholic mystic St. John of the Cross' "Dark Night of the Soul."*

I borrowed E. Allison Peer and St. Teresa of Silverio's edited and translated version from Burbank's Central Library stacks. Allison Peer's works were contemplated daily. I absorbed St. John's esoteric poetry. It described stages I recognized. Particularly the one I was experiencing. Release of sense attachments, those personal addictions to worldly needs, was underway. Alchemy of thought patterns and behaviors had begun.

Emotionally excruciating clearings rose up, requiring attention and courage beyond the physical recovery work I had accepted. A psychological de-construction orchestrated by spirit on my soul composed a death dirge. As I read the book, it illuminated. I better understood what I was in the midst of experiencing.

Two essential truths of transformative healing were present. My primary responsibility was to let go and just be with whatever came up. Surrender the need to plan or try to effect internal shifts. To accept that I had no control of the process. A secondary, though essential key was: I must still myself. My outer life became purposefully still and more solitary. The greatest challenge was to simply wait quietly and allow the process that was happening to happen.

Allison's translation revealed how we each experience soulful integration as it uniquely suits our journey. How our willfulness is broken down so soul may begin to lead. Spirit compassionately, at death's doorway, had left my much needed personal will intact. It allowed my courageous heart to reclaim living in a body and pursue full functionality. Embark upon my outer recovery work with the will of a warrior.

Now It whispered, "Good job, well done. Lay down your sword. Lift up your staff and follow me." I understood the invitation. A higher mercy had left me with what I needed—enough stamina to arrive at true surrender, yielding to Divine will. It would require a deepened level of courage. There was more work ahead. Resistant false self was still interfering.

Being temporarily disabled had been a gift. It stopped my hurried, "red alert" mentality and gave me the fresh look at life I had asked for. Focused connection with moment-to-moment experiences had been heavenly. It was a briefly lived Nirvana that I now knew existed. Its Realness had slowly faded as my brain rebooted and reconnected with my body. A fear-based programming had not been entirely deleted during stroke events. It slithered in a back door, while a new operating system was downloading in my brain. Right there alongside hard-earned awareness gifts, it resumed its fear inducing tactics. Buddhists call this mind-saboteur "monkey mind." Rick Carson's *Taming Your Gremlin®* introduced me to false-mind chatter years earlier. While hospitalized, unable to read, I sensed my horizontal environment was gremlin related. Saboteur/gremlin/ monkey-mind intellect was still industriously alive.

Adult Time Outs

The grem-monkey on my back was a two-ton gorilla. It wore cleats and stomped around. As it stirred things up, it policed me to be in a rush. Issuing orders was its favorite primate pastime. It was humorless and tricky. I watched, waited and breathed.

I coughed up a psychological hairball. Bones of emotional debris, remnants of what I had choked on for years, showed themselves. Spirit helped me breathe. Respiratory grace gave me strength and perseverance. I was encouraged to look through toxic bits and pieces to discover what had turned my life inside-out-upside-down. However stinky or distasteful unexamined habits and patterns seemed-felt, they were unflinchingly reviewed.

Process delivered the dramatically scripted movie that I'd been acting in my whole life. Roles, lines, players and props all lined up and made sense. I felt stirrings of freed energy to recreate my future. Two Ton had dropped substantial poundage. A sweetheart, soul voice reminded me to go outside. To touch ground. Earth Mother soothed my weeping, opened heart. Life became clearer from the inside out.

I noticed when old responses were reactivated by certain people, places and situational challenges. I felt tense, tight or tingling sensations in related chakra's area of my body. I breathed when I realized my breath was held. I understood emotional triggers were related to a "less than best" psychological aspect of me that I was learning to see clearly. Allowing space for its darkness to be alchemized by the elixir of Love was my charge. Awareness being 'Love's Light' beamed onto matters at hand. I reminded myself: *This too can be experienced with a completely expanded awareness.* Process work repeatedly reviewed misconceptions released or reframed untruths. Conscious creation of positive, resonant thoughts lovingly emerged.

To know Who We Are is often to first discover *who we are not.* Inner work exposed concepts—that became beliefs. Beliefs that I had been identified with. Release from their delusional traps smoothed out my life's playing field. I was able to refresh and renew consciously with clearer self-awareness.

While I was interviewing Carmen in 2011, she had commented, "You had to excavate. Heal your past."

"Yes," I'd said, "that's the word...*excavate.*"

I curiously wondered during and after the big release, "Who's voice is that?" when the saboteur gremlins acted out. They'd say something dismissive, or want me to hurt myself. I could hear them and simply listened. Daring me to trip in the shower and crack my skull, they were vicious in their last ditch efforts. That level of meanness has dissolved. The false self still pouts and moans when not taken seriously, sending fearful threats of danger if I do not hurry up and rush on with my life. It believes in death and fears it.

The gentleness of slowing down melted and salved heavy-handedness. I watched carefully, when false self snuck around. Making an enemy would have been counterproductive. Being the loving watcher became the only way to allow truth. I continue to listen and feel carefully, and pay attention with whole hearted full-bodied "sense-ability."

To excavate, or purge, was vital for my overall healing process. I dared to ask hard questions of my emotional memory. Kindly note before we go on, engaging with gremlin/saboteur is counterproductive—not recommended in the least.

While watching sly habitual chatter of grem-monkey mind, I investigated a shadowy inner being. Hidden in dungeon darkness,

I'd shine my light with no disagreement or judgment. "Who are you?" I inquired with reverent listening. "I want to embrace the gift of you. Your fierce adamancy has something to share. Tell me what's beneath that sad anger." Deep inner work was honored with contemplative adult time outs.

Powerful visualization exercises in Jacqueline Small's *Awakening in Time* helped me view, process and describe shadow qualities I had been working at uncovering my entire adult life. E-mail's *vacation response* option was activated often. Solitude morphed into inner sanctuary. Grace's healing insights bubbled up.

Purification felt liberating. Spirit guided me to Northern California for a self-administered weekend retreat. The fireplace in Asilomar's older accommodations warmed my body during this Pacific Grove respite. I watched whales play on Monterrey Bay. Enjoyed nature walks witnessing evening feeding deer. I sipped tea read and wrote in a small main-street coffee house. A lender book's title caught my eye, so I sat down and read a few pages of *Veils of Separation*. I loved Rabia Erduman's storytelling style of our integrative process. I down loaded her e-book once I returned home. In perfect time, I was realizing an integral ingredient of my recent inner work.

In its essence, it was my wounded inner child's reclamation. I thought I had done this work before. Clearly there had been more to do. Who I discovered while doing Smalls' visualization work, cowering in the deepest regions of my heart, was a scared little girl with tears on her face.

After all that had passed, I made generous space for Self-honoring. Re-parenting little Antoinette was practiced with tenderness. Offering her love and appreciation, hearing her childish worries, reassuring her we will always be safe. I knew her tearful fears needed to be released. Their origin's emotional wounds are what had made me sick, almost killed me. I promised her to always be full of care. She would always have me.

Natural born gifts and talents were reclaimed along with little me's wounded heart power. They bubbled up as long ignored loves and interests awakened. I felt a curiosity and wonderment with life.

Truth I learned: What lies beneath the muck and mire are precious diamonds. Diamonds in the rough, waiting to be mined, ready to be polished and set to benefit us All. Contribute on multitudinous levels. For me, they began to shine in earnest the more I yielded to my true heart's song. Artist Donna Iona Drozda's *Luna See* website wisdom highlights my experience: *"Move through this particular wisdom cycle—with openness to your shadow side. Recognize that what you gain from relationship with its needs will lead to something—wonderfully liberating."*

Allowing ego-personality to be assimilated in to my soulful Heart *was* the process. We began turning around long-held beliefs. I felt empowered to make fresh choices once the emotional storm quieted. Many revisions were simply a love-based version of an old concept or belief. I understood the juncture I was at. I had surrendered to the best of my ability. Soul was in charge.

The need for an outer coach ended in March 2010. I wrote Janaki saying I would miss our work together. It felt a little weird going solo. It was time for me to leave the nest and rely on spiritual wings. I had deeply realized: none of us are ever alone. Being children of the Universe, we are never spiritually abandoned. I committed to self-nurturing and honoring what I now knew.

Earlier that year, Janaki had sent a coaching reply e-mail which included a note: *"You have a way with words, Antoinette—have you noticed?"* Her thoughtful question encouraged a personal inquiry. I let it gestate for a while. I sensed in my heart that it was true.

I basked in the fresh air of revitalization. Breathing and noticing a lot of work had gone on those past three years, I declared: Break Time. At a near-by thrift shop, I picked out summer items for my reclaimed inner child. She had brought a playful curiosity back to us. We took a plane south. It was her first invitation to relax with me and be cared for in my little retreat by the sea. She asked me to give her vacation backpack and colorful attire to Angel Notion, so a little Mayan girl might enjoy playing in them, too. Her generosity and quick-to-smile nature softened my serious adult's features.

She'd always been within me, this little magical child. At St. Joe's it was her child-like eagerness I tapped into while learning everything again. Once emotionally imprisoned, she is no longer my inner brat. She listens as well as teaches me how to play, a little bit more each day. She feels safe and cared for. Her freed energy returns me to my innocence, purifying my inner young adult's insistent 'mean-Levine' act. Not needing to take care of everyone and everything, I had finally stopped making life into a serious drama, a problem to be solved. I felt relieved, yet remained observant. Increased creative energy relaxed my mind. Generosity tickled me pink.

A loving thought popped in: Theresa's school spring break was approaching. I invited her, the first family member to join me in Mexico. We shared a week of my fourteen days in Playa del Carmen. It was a delightful love-fest, Fuzzy Wuzzy and Granny Goose playtime. We'd not had recreational, adult-sister time for decades. It was a gift we gave one another. We both got slightly sunburned as well.

She enjoyed meeting and dining with Anuar and Waldo during lively conversation on their roof top terrace. Theresa's wisdom words: "Find your fun and do it." Another simple truth I learned and embraced. Bliss revival was long overdue.

Sowing the Seeds of Love…

Jessica Tuck, producer and co-founder of the spoken-word series 'Spark Off Rose', extended an invitation. Founded in 2001, its mission is to create community through the art of storytelling. September 2010's theme was "Air." My telling story joined nine others. We wrote our fascinating, hilarious, touching "Air"-related pieces, rehearsed and readied ourselves.

Our Monday night presentation at Santa Monica's Powerhouse Theater arrived. I waited backstage in the little theatre's makeshift green room, listening to fellow storytellers until it was my turn. Then I removed my comfy Merrill flats and exchanged them for Kenneth Cole ankle-strap platforms.

A self-selected forty seconds of Tears for Fears rhythms cued me on stage. "Sowing the Seeds of Love" introduced my storytelling. Friends, coaching colleagues and clients joined in the audience's welcoming applause. I sat in a chair, spine erect, and inhaled deeply. I spoke clearly and strongly, filled with focus and intent. I did not stand up, until I demonstrated rising from a St. Joe's hospital wheelchair.

It was an exhilarating and interesting experience. No egg on my face or mud on my shoes. Audience comments given at the event's reception varied. Once friend's hellos and hugs quieted, other audience members approached. "Keep sharing your *'it's an inside job'* story," they said. Like-heart and like-minded folks smiled. Others wanted to know how the lupus was doing. Still learning the art of levity, I missed an opportunity for a humorous reply.

I had contemplated relaxing quietly somewhere nearby, before and after the event to stay away from bumper-to-bumper, hour-plus commutes across the LA basin. Quality energy for a very public night was my heart's desire. Linda recommended a quaint Venice inn. A drive up the coast the next morning was also a possibility. A quiet repose after months of writing and rewriting might be nice. It would be. After a good night's sleep, I headed north up Pacific Coast Highway 1 to where a room waited for me at the Venice inn's sister location.

Being ocean side with a garden view, I never turned on the television. I wanted silence. I walked the fine sand at the ocean's edge and watched pipers peck for meals. Offering appreciation for all that had been. I felt the storytelling event had been a going public with my unique perspective resulting from inimitable experiences. I felt nonplused in a peculiar way— thinking I would have felt inclined to advance onward with coaching. Yet I didn't feel that way at all. I spent two peaceful nights, meditating on the crash and hush of near-by waves. I began asking myself with journal entries what I wanted in Life, writing from my heart with truthful wonderings.

My health had improved exponentially with inner work. When Janaki had asked, "What if this dis-ease is always with you?" I replied, "Then it must be what I came here to be with."

At a recent St. Joe's Young Stroke Survivor's gathering, I was asked if I feared reoccurring strokes. I wholeheartedly offered, "No, I don't treat myself the way I used to." I had divorced victimhood. Fear of unexpected bodily harm was no longer my reality. Higher perspectives were on the rise, recreating my life and health. Fear was losing its stronghold.

An excerpt from the September 13th speaking event is telling:

"I no longer victimize myself. I stopped identifying lupus as 'my lupus.' I have no ownership of it, only care and responsibility for my body. As evidence of disease continues to shrink, I treat myself with gentle reverence and cooperate with my well-being."

The discontinued steroid prednisone and its pharmaceutical side effects were clearing out my body's eco-system. A milder medication was prescribed, with its doses reduced every three to six months. My colorful, two-week vita-med box contained vitamins, mineral supplements and one prescription drug. It had been a three-year-combined traditional/alternative healing process.

I had never believed in a "pill fairy." I was ultimately responsible to honor my body-temple and life. Vibrant organic foods and a moderately active lifestyle sustained my ever-improving health. My emerging self wanted to enjoy life's gifts as well as offer compassionate guidance to others.

I was not overly enthused or inspired to grow a coaching practice. A participant in a Mastering Your Craft tele-course with *Taming Your Gremlin®* author Rick Carson, I had an inkling that coaching may not be my craft. Not in its classic form, at least. I listened as worldwide participants (social workers, doctors, coaches and lawyers) participated and shared.

Energetically, I felt positive community resonance. But maybe my authentic craft was elsewhere. I received spontaneous guidance from Rick during one session. I blurted out my fear: *to commit to writing a book.*

My aspiration scared me, though I had shared it with Jessica Tuck during our "Air" producer-writer alliance meetings. A recently viewed Wayne Dyer "Excuses Be Gone" DVD inspired me. Modeling his visionary advice, I found an unused hardback book, reversed the cover and wrote "My First Book" in magenta-Sharpie ink. It sat out loud in plain view.

Burbank Adult School's upcoming schedule arrived in the mail. I usually tossed it in the recycling bin, but I was in student mode. Yes, indeed, it included fiction and non-fiction writing classes. I registered for Cynthia Friedlob's ten-week course. A retired television series script editor, she provided insights. My rising desire to write an inspirational book became better informed.

True creative surprise would show itself a little later. Cynthia prompted our writing assignments with artful images. One was of a man and woman sitting in a vintage apartment living room. My make-believe Canadian artist character wanted to resume painting. From Quebec, she now lived in a 1939 New York flat with her husband. Her cousins, whom she missed dearly, lived in Saskatchewan. She had disowned her gifts of artistry and her accomplished attendance at the Paris Sorbonne.

Thus I spun a fictitious tale loosely mirroring elements of my life. Writing helped me process them. From time to time surrenders on the page have led to liberating 'let go's' in real life. To make a short story even shorter: in real life, my little condo in Playa which also doubles as an income property became interwoven with my fictional artist's tale. The death of an upcoming vacation rental guest caused the need to give an unanticipated cash refund...to an actual person from Saskatchewan. Living on a limited income at that time, I was learning to trust the natural flow of resources. I wasn't contractually obliged to return a newly widowed Saskatchewan woman $1,800. USD Still in a state of shock she said, "I will not be going on vacation for awhile." Her husband, who had booked my place, had suffered a sudden fatal heart attack. She called from Canada explaining something that required no explanation whatsoever. I heard her grief and spent moments listening to her telling story. In silent gratitude, I sent her love and appreciation for the opportunity to be in my heart and gently witness another's suffering. She kindly accepted my request to return the monies over time. I was a bit squeamish to send it all at once, as "money story" gremlin was still being tamed.

Within a month a gentleman from Quebec booked the cancelled dates plus a few more for $2,400. He and his wife are now return guests for two months in 2012. God doeth work in mysterious ways.

The writing process is only one of the ways Source demonstrated and taught me laws of abundance. Its soft, giving nature inspired my growing trust. Relationships with all manner of life's situations shifted and thrived. Some died, if they were at their end. A relaxed heart-mind showed me new choices and morphed lingering attachments. A DirecTV contract I had maintained from the 2009 move was cancelled. Initially, it felt weird giving up an old favorite pastime, surfing with a remote control in hand. In the end, television viewing habits weren't missed. The void it created opened up time and space for other interests. DVDs with funny, poignant and inspired plots were viewed upon occasion. Spiritual Cinema Circle's monthly mailing of inspired films replaced a Netflix subscription. Conscious choices felt good.

Superior guidance led to a new spontaneity. Dr. Rogal's ironic humor in a 2007 counseling session—"*You need to plan to be more spontaneous*"—had been taken to heart. My trust fund grew as my intentions manifested.

I felt ready to move on figuratively and literally. The one-year lease on the 1939 Spanish house would soon expire. Since I'd sold the condo, I felt free to live anywhere that called to me. My vision was bigger than my pocketbook at this point. But I held a space in my heart for a house in the woods, with views of starlit skies. Ancient growth trees and moonlit darkness in the absence of city lights. For the time being I recreated a "my home" wish list I'd written while selling the condo. It had added clarity of vision for realization of the 1939 house. New descriptions pointed to a smaller, simpler house equally as serene. I set it aside.

Recognizing that tremendous inner work and corresponding outer shifts had been experienced, I slowed down that winter. A graceful minimizing of coach-client alliances began. New Year's 2011 found me relaxed in my Yucatan Peninsula home away from home, my once-comatose body rejuvenated by sunrise yoga salutations on Caribbean fine white sands.

Fifth Life Process

Fifth chakra process represents our life's challenge to unify individual will with Divine will. Surrendering ego's willfulness to Source is a seeker's ultimate quest. *'Thy Will, not mine, be done'* is the sacred truth and energy calling of this stage.

Located at our throat, fifth chakra energy governs our thyroid gland, trachea, esophagus and neck vertebrae, as well as our jaw mouth and teeth. Balanced fifth chakra mind-emotion qualities are reflected in our self-expression and creative interaction. This stage's energy regulates our co-creative ability. When it is energized by heart power and grounded with lower chakra support, our capabilities extend beyond fulfillment of our basic needs. Stage Five's energy activates inspired creativity as we bring *consciousness* to personal interactions and communication.

This stage's process evolves and integrates into our Being as we further ground ourselves in alignment with Source energy. It governs our abilities to creatively express in unison with Divine will. Imbalanced Stage Five energy demonstrates as creative stagnation, obsessive behavior and lack of expressiveness.

Our mind-emotion's Stage Four lessons arrive through 'power of choice' challenges. Stage Five evolves us to allow Divine direction as our primary authority, as we surrender our willfulness and accept the sacred power of this stage. We become spiritually empowered as we surrender to Source as our superior guide. Conscious connection with Divine direction, while being personally empowered—respecting our free will, is our paradoxical challenge.

Learning to resonate with Source, we are called to intuitively enlist choices that reflect higher perspectives. We learn to trust divine guidance, watching, waiting and listening for our best next steps. Worldview instructions of how to achieve our life's goals contradict fifth chakra's sacred truth. We are programmed to struggle, work hard to achieve desired results; this is often our habitual way of accomplishment. Honoring Stage Five truth challenges our entrenched habits of achievement.

Aligning with Our True Power

Our Stage Five quest is to evolve beyond lower-center's concepts of authority. In this process, we surrender the influences maintained by our family of origin, society and our ego-oriented will. Ideally, we gain complete independence from previous definitions of power. Our spiritual goal is consistent alignment with Source, including inspired right-choice and right-action guidance. As in every stage's conscious expansion of our energy, we relinquish fear-based aspects of ego's personality, yielding and allowing a Creative force to operate through us.

Our alignment with this center's co-creative gift relies on the strength of our conscious grounding, self-understanding, trust and integrity.

Spiritually matured, we honor our thoughts, words and deeds, and communicate with impeccable integrity. Thus, we are empowered to consciously participate in a Universal co-creative process. We are called forth to accept full responsibility for the manner in which we utilize our willpower.

We realize it is a Divinity inside us, granting us creative capabilities to manifest outcomes beyond those previously known. With appreciation for our role in the co-creative process, we respect the Invisible power that our thought-emotion energy generates. In all manner of creative endeavors and interactions, be they simple tasks or complex expressions, we recognize a limitless capacity to manifest. We grow and learn to take responsibility for our co-creator energy.

Fifth chakra's relative openness empowers our conscious co-creative choice *or* the inevitable consequences of unconscious decisions. The power of both means of creation rests in this center's open or blocked energy state. Fifth Stage process's truth demonstrates that our spiritually guided personal power, led by Divine will, empowers us to co-create meaningful self-expressions. The quality of our manifestations is reliant on our relative alignment with Source.

We Welcome Divine Guidance

As fifth chakra energy balances, surrendered personal will cooperates with unfolding co-creative elements. We learn to accept every detail as Divine guidance. Ego-centric resistance to God's undeterminable timing lessens. Our response to life's details shifts. We notice a subtle nuance of patterns as connective steps unfold. We learn to release our limited way of doing things and surrender to the Unlimited directive that flows from Life. Our curiosity and imaginative nature reawakens, one day at a time, breath to breath.

Our ability to *yield*, give way *to what is* moment to moment, influences this center's creative energy. As we recognize and acknowledge the divine insights and symbols that active sixth chakra energy reveals to us, Divine guidance becomes the only course we follow. This is fifth chakra wisdom at its best.

Our co-creative ability expands as our alignment with Source energy remains consistent. Spiritual and personal power unify as we honor our co-creative capability with humble reverence for Divine process. Previously seen as separate, our spiritual and personal lives are experienced as one in the same. We honor our inner and outer life's unified sovereignty feeling empowered to fully express our unique talents and gifts. Inspired to experiment, we allow our imagination to be increasingly active in a focused manner, following our true heart's guidance.

Co-creation is Our Divine Right

Opened fifth chakra energy empowers our creative intent. We are able to have an unlimited dream of what is possible in our life. Our Self-acceptance, matured by Stage Four's heart reclamation, allows us to recognize co-creation as a Divine right. Stage Five offers a sacred invitation to wield an unperceivable power. Knowing a power greater than our self is within us, our spiritual responsibility of right use remains a constant. Respect for conscious intention is a core principal that reflects this responsibility.

Our increased ability to remain centered in heart power, supported by regular breath work meditative practices, bolsters our conscious intent. Self-reflective, contemplative study—while honoring the process of revisiting lingering issues—strengthens our co-operation in a sacred co-creative partnership. Self-respecting alliance with Source is our greatest strength.

We have reached a stage where we are certain we are more than our physical body. We know our spiritual Heart is our essence. We experience conscious connection with manifestation of life's circumstances. Our committed self-examination has helped clear up inner dissonance and unconscious patterns of mind-emotion energy. The iron shavings that blocked our heart's magnetic power are falling away, opening us to the possibilities of Stage Five's co-creative energy. If not fully readied, we courageously review and release faulty thought patterns in exchange for loving thoughts that nurture instead of destroy our precious co-creative energy.

Traversing the Energetic Heart-Mind Bridge

Our throat's fifth chakra location, between our heart and our mind, indicates a sacred bridge. Co-creative energy resonates between our fourth and sixth chakra centers. At this stage's opening, the free flow of heart energy and mind energy is significant. We begin to notice our thoughts and related feeling responses. As we consciously recognize the energy quality of inner promptings, our thought-emotion frequencies are deliberately filtered through our fifth chakra's energy of intentional choice.

We capably delve into self-inquiry, asking from our heart/mind: Is my perceptive a Higher Self ideal of loving energy? Am I experiencing ego fear-based thoughts? What would be my purest intention in this moment?

We purposely want to allow spirit to recover our authentic choices, such that they are grounded in the wisdom of our fourth, fifth and sixth chakra centers: all-inclusive love, yielding to *what is* —from proactive inspired choice. Realizing Self-empowered choice governs our ability to create meaningful expressions and circumstances.

Meeting Stage Five's Challenges

As Stage Five evolves, fear-based patterns of control remain our greatest challenge. A heightened level of conscious awareness *n o t i c e s* when ego's control urges are active. Attempts at control are ego's unconscious competition with Higher Authority. Stage Five's open energy, recognizes that unconscious leanings have co-opted our true heart's energy long enough, and gently witnesses ego's shenanigans with love.

The grace of aligning our energy with Source allows us to notice and choose a more resonant, empowering thought. Empowered awareness chooses thoughts that feel good from a higher loving perspective.

Attempts to take over a divine process hamper its flow. Acting out of fear creates resistant energy that derails our highest intentions. Our efforts will feel tiresome, akin to hard work. Our spiritual practices can become contaminated as well. Overuse of our personal will with meditation, self-introspection and other practices is less productive and potentially harmful to our well being. We are seeking heart-mind balance, which calls for inspired use of our free will.

By now, it is clear that our Stage Five challenge is linked to our relative alignment with Source energy. Any shadow of self-doubt, self-importance, or belief it is our charge to handle outcomes without

Divine grace interferes. Lower energy fear-based thoughts require our conscious attending to, in order to unblock the pure energy flow of consciousness. We calmly reevaluate the quality of intent, reviewing the motivation behind our decisions.

Fifth chakra energy calls us to be the keepers of our integrity, and signals us when we have slipped below our higher values and knowledge of goodness. When our motivation was strictly for personal gain at the detriment or lack of concern for others, we take a closer look at our ideal standard. We become responsible for our co-creative energy with pure intentions and inspired actions. We make our way to higher choices of what is good for all concerned, while turning outcomes over to a Higher Authority.

Conscious Forgiveness and Making Amends

Open flow of fifth chakra energy empowers our ability to consciously apologize for any wrongful use of our word or will. Immoral acts or any behavior less than our personal code of honor are considered false and faulty. Our ability to make amends and acknowledge we have been dishonorable strengthens our integrity.

Fifth chakra energy invites us to release judgment and critical self-diminishment. Our recognition of *who we are* settles for nothing less than loving witnessing. We regain an authentic humbleness as spirit guides us to higher intentions.

Self-forgiveness arises as open fourth chakra energy infuses fifth's with the energy that empowers choice to be non-judgmental. As we gain respect for our original, unspoiled Nature, we cannot help but forgive. Through self-forgiveness and making amends with others, we consistently reclaim our spirits from misdirected willfulness. We become able to course-correct with grace and ease. Spirit guides our best intentions, leading us toward full expression of our authentic Self.

Choosing to Trust

Our Intention to be Centered is our constant companion as we fully commit to receiving the benefits of our journey. We return again and again to our heart center as we grow to accept and trust our conscious choices—realizing that whatever the temporary outcome is, if our action was well intended, it will lead to our next best step. Faith becomes trust in a Divine process of co-creation. Joyful trust emerges when we notice our higher consciousness improves our ability to choose. Ease of effort becomes the norm as we gain an ability to focus our mind on intentional choices, ones that noticeably correlate with improved outcomes.

We realize our intentional role in the changes we witness. Our power of intentional choice is invigorated by our ability to consciously trust. We understand that if our faithful trust is misdirected by keeping our attention on less-than-beneficial circumstances, unwanted outcomes will continue to unfold. This understanding leads us to an appreciation for the energy of Trust and the importance of *how* we focus our attention.

Self-responsibility, our ability to respond with higher loving consciousness, is a key quality of Stage Five's co-creative energy. Guided by our consciously developed sense of responsibility, we recognize our power is reliant on the quality of our intentional attention. Our attention is partnered with our trust in a Divine creative process. The combination of these two gives us access to right use of personal will.

Now, our intentional attention becomes energized by heart power, which gives us the necessary courage to accept Stage Five's inspiration and empowerment. When our conscious mind focuses with love, we allow Creative Principle to express through us. We begin to detach from ego-centric survival mode and fear-based perspectives and actions. We become more fascinated with partaking in activity inspired by invisible Grace, recognizing our successes are results of our higher state of consciousness. Our patience level matures from our trust in divine outcomes. While trusting our heartfelt intentions, we quietly watch for signs and symbols to guide us on, listening to our still, small voice's intuitive messages and prompts.

Dissolving Resistance to Change through Surrender

Allowance of Divine guidance shines a light on the pitfalls of our maturing co-creative relationship. An emotional desire for change may be in conflict with a psychological resistance to change. Fifth chakra empowerment helps us surrender intellectual fear to our heart's power of intentional choice. We surrender old concepts of power so that we may receive true power. It can appear as a scary notion, when viewed from all we were taught about achievement in life. The ultimate truth of Divine power courageously accepted, however, unblocks our forward movement. Willingly, we proceed with micro-movements or inspired big steps that lead to an enlivened life.

Our spiritual goal is to be an instrument, an expression of Source. At last, we are empowered to manifest in absence of a willful interpretation of what we need to do. We learn to release control accepting, trusting that *we will be shown*. Our job is to *listen and follow* guidance given us by our spiritual Heart with non-attachment to results.

Surrendering to pure consciousness matures our friendship with life's Mystery. Trust in the unknowable, unquantifiable nature of Source energy is our responsible choice. And with this, we recognize that we do not know how or when "right time" will be revealed to us. We allow God's timing. We observe situational shifts when unblocked energy transforms the body of our life. Until we relinquish all obstructive attitudes, we vacillate between awe of the co-creative process and ego's disappointed need to control.

Fruits of Fifth Chakra Energy

Our willingness to surrender, to yield to the flow of what is, allows co-creative empowerment. A nonjudgmental, lovingly detached nature enhances our strengthened choice-making ability. Our healthy, detached energy is less constricted by concerns for outer results. We are focused on a continued commitment to alignment, union with Source. Whichever direction our soulful presence chooses, it is anchored in a higher consciousness. We see life through eyes of love. Joy reigns supreme as we recognize our true intrinsic nature.

Capable of enjoying the beauty and wonderment of what surrounds us, we enjoy life's passing pleasures with grace and ease. Realization that we are here as co-creators with Source shifts our need to hold on, emboldens our belief in abundance. Our all-inclusive love and ability to forgive energy bank fuels our creative ability. We think with our heart.

Generosity of Heart colors our choice-making as we experience an expanded level of creativity. '*My cup runneth over*' expresses our great gratitude. We experience and respect a wizard-like artistry in our relationship with Divine power. Our appreciation and gratitude for Divine guidance is upheld by Self appreciation.

Beneficially, we regain authentic humility as we experience spirit's guidance. Capable of wise decision-making, we intentionally commit to our choices, equally capable to course-correct when deemed necessary. We become the artist of our life circumstances as we create from centered fourth chakra energy. Joined with sixth chakra (Higher Mind) wisdom we become free of worldly definitions of success and failure, we grow confident beyond need for outer sanctioning of our inspired direction of choice. Universal beauty and order of unfolding are acknowledged from our wizened perspective.

When Stage Five's challenges are met, we hear the words of the Serenity Prayer as truth and accept responsibility for our divinely guided choices. Our courageous Heart *accepts the things it cannot change and changes the things it can, wisely understanding the difference.*

Fifth Self-Inquiry

Here we are. A little pause and some
s l o w i n g   d o w n with long deep breaths
always feels good. Enjoy some as you settle
in comfortably for self introspection.

~How do I use my willpower? How does this affect me? How does
it affect my relations with others?

~Am I authentic in my personal expressions? If not, how do I mask
my true self? Describe what you uncover:

~ When I am dishonest or inauthentic, how does this affect my ability to collaborate with others?

~ To whom do I give my allegiance of authority? What force of power controls my life?

~ What control issues do I still struggle with? What disrupts or blocks my connection with Source?

~ What personal issues do I most need to reevaluate that cloud my conscious understanding of life?

~ Do I trust in Higher Self guidance or do I attempt to take charge of outcomes on my own? What, if anything, do I want to change about this?

~ Do I trust signs and signals of divine guidance? Am I consistently capable of following spontaneous prompts, with no knowledge of where they will lead?

~ What fear patterns do I fall back into most often? How do I behave when this occurs?

~ What patterns of willful resistance do I recognize in my personality? Would I describe myself as stubborn or obstinate?

~ Have I addressed healing my emotional attachments to harmful habits and patterns? What do I use as emotional crutches in my daily life?

Now is an opportune moment to utilize 'Micro Moves'. Peaceful blessings . . .

TRUTH FLOW...

Be a lamp or

a lifeboat or a ladder.

Help someone's soul heal.

Walk out of your house,

like a shepherd.

RUMI

Sixth Inspiration

Brother-friend, sobriety role model, Joseph had sent me an e-mail in early October 2010. For me, at this time surrender had morphed into joy of Being. Our correspondence clarified my purposeful direction.

Joseph wrote:

"I do not believe my current recovery from alcohol would have lasted long enough for a true fighting chance had it not been for your near-death experiences. When I took my last drink, it was 06-01-2006.

If you recall, I was sitting in downtown's Seattle Best Coffee that day in November 2006 when you just happened to walk in. How amazing that you would be staying in the hotel attached to my refuge spot during and after my homelessness.

I was eventually placed in a program that provided transitional housing. My life had become more comfortable than it had been in five years.

As the months went on, I failed to balance my multiple recovery-based activities and began isolating. Historically when I have fallen back in isolation, I relapse.

However, this time I received frightening news. You were in a coma. Though I was restricted by the courts to travel out of state, my mental health counselor said he would advocate hard before it was too late.

The heart of this message is your life-threatening situation and my semi-recovered state gave me the strength of will and extreme motivation to redouble my commitment to myself.

In retrospect, another great gift I received as a result of the way the weave was woven was this: I learned that we don't need to be somewhere physically to 'be there'."

I replied:

"Joseph, my dearest brother-friend…I *heard* your July 2007 e-mail while I silently fought for life.

While in hospital, I was given updates on your recovery that made my heart soar, and furthered my recognition that I too was in a recovery process.

I had recently, before the 'Air' storytelling event, invoked the release of deeply hidden addictive habits and psychological patterns. An earthquake erupted in my psyche. It was further fueled by telling my 'return to life' story in front of 100 people.

My addiction to control's hidden anger almost took my life. My recovery journey continues to shrink old insane behaviors, thought processes, fears and doubts. And like the wicked witch in Wizard of Oz….they're crying out…'I'm melting…I'm melting…'

I learned how to trust and love myself exactly as I am.

Thank you for your contribution to this unfolding, this blossoming of the real me.

We both lived and remembered who-we-really-are through what almost took our lives. And share it with others. Every day I give thanks and deepen ownership and offering of my gifts. My heart rejoices that you do as well.

I recognize my true identity as an infinite Being. Put here on Mother Earth at this time, right here, right now.

Always sending you unconditional love. Thank you for your timely letter and self-expressed way of being."

Gentleness...

Simplicity is what Lama Lhanang Rinpoche might offer. The lush, semi-tropic grounds of Jardin Shangri-La were to host his four-day Playa del Carmen workshop. Sheila, a local amiga, taught kundalini yoga in the garden's circular activity center. Waist-level screens allowed drifts of plant-generated air to refresh the cavernous space. Flyers for his workshop had caught my attention while attending her class. It felt like an inviting entry to a new year.

Tibetan yoga techniques and talks rounded out Lama's presence. I still utilize the march-in-place arm-swing cardio moves he taught us whenever I relish the benefits of cardio movement on land or in the house. Listening to his talks validated my experiences. My authentic self was emerging. Good.

New Year's Eve 2011 dinner and companionship were scrumptious. Our meal was prepared and presented by, George a chef friend of Anuar and Waldo. I shared several meals with Esther Raventos and Robert Berlin of Toronto, neighbor owners in Playa, on their third-story unit's balcony terrace overlooking our complex's lush garden courtyard. Pool lights glowed while we sipped Spanish wine. As Esther and Robert are both intellectuals, our conversations were laced with bright Canadian humor and U.S. politic. Having noticed a change in my temperament, Robert remarked, "You've really gone Zen." I joined in the laughter, humming a chuckle and relaxing in the balmy night air.

I enjoyed these two weeks of visits with friends. Pre-dawn solo seaside yoga connected me with inner and outer Life and commenced my relaxed days at home. A jump in the chilled pool water and a few short exhilarating laps followed. These were my morning practices before Jose, the groundskeeper, began upkeep at eight. Then I savored a breakfast of fresh tropical fruits and yogurt, sat beneath my patio umbrella and wrote.

Lama Rinpoche's guidance had been right to the point. "Heal and help yourself. First." I'd shared a few sentences of my little story, mentioning internal questions about intuitive coaching efforts. He acknowledged the kindness and generosity he saw in me then added, "You are too sensitive." Three weeks later, back in the states, I understood better what he meant.

It was explained to me. Oft times an expanded energy field comes with return-to-life and other traumatic experiences. Resultant hypersensitivity can be common. A mastered guide, whom I connect with annually, interpreted the Lama's brevity. He proposed, "You've experienced God, you've experienced Compassion, but you are still afraid of It. You think It will hurt you. Let go the trauma, learn to resonate with the Energy. It's what brought you back to life."

I felt humbled by my lapse in receiving the benefits of transformative experiences. I wanted to be, beyond this phase of opening up. And I also understood timing wasn't up to me. My job was to co-operate fully, release resistance. Wisdom teacher's books were reread for their helpful descriptions of becoming whole. I often unplugged letting calls go to voicemail, and e-mail wait. A deepened silence and stillness returned as I honored process. *"Make friends with the Invisible. Embrace compassionate self-care"* was the higher self-guidance I received.

Tanya's YMCA kundalini yoga class was an instrumental clearing practice. Connecting with community helped me stay grounded, while yoga focused my integrative energy work. I rode waves of spontaneous tears of emotional release on the mat. Shameless revisits lit up small pockets of sorrow, while insights burst through showing me conditioned mind patterns that nearly destroyed my body. Self-for-giving Love eased and soothed my open heart. I rolled up my mat and blanket with a quiet smile. Spirit reassembled my mind-body week to week, strengthening my lightness of being while navigating my body's healing.

Medication doses reduced further as blood tests remained stable, pleasing Dr. Lee and me as I flirted with remission of a systemic lupus condition.

I understood the messages I was receiving. One's intention to be of service must be balanced with self-nurturing. Selflessness balanced with healthy selfishness. I had to review what I really wanted in life, again.

Coaching clients in person had an element of energy drain. Practicing it wasn't as freeing and revitalizing as I had imagined. CTI's coaches' training had been an enormous gift, enhancing interpersonal skills and providing a brilliant co-active model for what I felt drawn to teach and practice. I realized my original decision was driven by a need to do something outwardly contributory. Now I felt my vocational inquiry turn inward. *What is my truest passion?* opened my heart-mind to further question and contemplate what I love doing.

Moments with Lama Rinpoche revealed an aversion, a fear I sensed in my gut. I'd finished our talk with, "Maybe it's time to write a book." He smiled, gathered his robes to exit Jardin Shangri-La's center and continue his day.

Anxiety dissonance had dampened my energy while I considered the unknown. Osho wrote that psychological fear is a fact of life. Those who face their fear, while being afraid but not paralyzed, are truly living. I felt enlivened reading his text, remembering my lifetime of tried and true courage. Resonating with heartfelt guidance it was time to decide and act.

A phone call to CTI refunded the advanced deposit I'd paid for their certification program. I released a need to have a recognized identity---a credential. I knew that writing must continue. It inspires refreshes and frees me as I honor it as an inborn gift.

Back in 2010, Regina had mentioned Natalie Goldberg's book, *Writing Down the Bones.* A copy arrived via priority mail from Better World Books, a literacy advocate and online bookstore. Goldberg's grounded Zen-like "get on with it" sensibility was exactly what I needed to absorb. Writing practice taught a way to connect with intuitive creation. Her descriptive "wild mind" was the real me waiting to be expressed. With a lessening of distractive mental noise, I felt freed to move forward more easily.

February 2011, the month of the heart, offered another opportunity to write and speak. Providence Saint Joseph's all-age stroke folk's support group coordinator asked me to present as a guest speaker and former participant. A lyrical piece flowed through my pen one silent morning while still in my warm bed. "Gentleness" was its title. It offered what my events taught me to remember. Young and not-so-young participants, including an aging Catholic nun, attended. I spoke of our Buddha Christ nature, our intrinsic Greatness. I was learning to be authentically uncensored. Heart-to-heart soul talk resonated. Sister gently set her hand on my arm and smiled kind words before leaving at the groups' conclusion. A caretaker assisted her as she exited utilizing a walker.

Lisa Armstrong and D'vorah Epstein came in support of all present. Held in 5 North's dining room, long tables formed a rectangular group setting. Lisa later sent an appreciative email, a reply to my "thank you" to her for attending. "I loved how you noted a correlation between our under-recognized adult gifts being talents we enjoyed when we were young. And connected with each attendee personally and invited them to share." And share they did. We all have a story. As I witnessed a pouring out of human greatness, its spirit filled the room.

A Reservation for Goldberg's March writing-yoga-meditation retreat was solidified. Four of my favorite being-doing balance practices—travel, write, yoga, meditate—were on the horizon. Housed in the stone and mortar of Taos New Mexico's Mabel Dodge-Luhan House, I was blessed by a synchronistic pairing. Sandra Campbell, published Canadian author, and I shared a high-ceilinged cottage. We each had our own quarters. Our lengthy kitchen offered views of Taos sunrises. Thirty women and one male professor sat, moved, wrote, read and ate for a week. The experience of meeting authors and other budding writers anchored purpose and bolstered courage. Sandra noted during one of our late night cottage confabs that my intended book might want to be from a 'what I learned' voice. The idea resonated with my evolving vision of the book.

During a desert van ride to Albuquerque airport at the retreat's end, I was accompanied by Diane Heath, a Reiki practitioner and 'thesacredordinary' Blogspot wizardress. A burst of enthusiasm ensued as I shared with Diane hints and clues about the book's shape: alphabet, numbers and colors were in its content. I imagined the book was to be the ABCs-123s of a joy-filled life. Spirit is funny. It transmitted the exact organizing tools needed to contain ideas that flooded and floated in. ABC-123s, seven chakra's colors and Sharpie felt-tip pens created beauty and order along the way as this book's grew.

Writing is a continuum of what I began long ago. I had submitted poetry to a 1960s version of *Kid's Life* magazine. Mailed passionate letters to the opinion editor at the *Pasadena Star News* while in high school. Business efforts had dominated my pen and keyboard for twenty-odd years. Off and on, I formed writing groups. One of the photos Jessica had taped at my hospital bedside reflects those starts. WOW—Write on, Women—monthly gatherings had been held under my condo's living room skylight.

Co-creative mode was becoming a new normal. Solutions, directions and the dance of balanced being-doing appeared. Intentional, gentle consistent self-witnessing led the way. Life became a *waking mediation*. Noticing where how and what my hands and eyes where focused on in the moment. Breathing into ordinary movements in a yogic-like manner felt marvelously centering. With grace and ease, I felt vibrantly present. Then I began to delve deeply into traumatic events of the recent past.

This message came through—voice recorded—while hiking up in Wildwood Canyon. It was what I most needed to hear. I had been feeling a little off kilter. It counseled me during a time when I had been sorting through reams of hospital reports and wound photos, a whole new level of emotional "too much." Spirit uplifted my heart and spoke, soft and clear:

"Allow it to come through you, Antoinette. When you write about the past, it is essential that you remain grounded. Very present, very self-caring, absolutely present in your soulful Heart. You are loved. Treat yourself well, kindly and gently. You can be with this."

I strengthened my conscious connection with Heart Self, by monitoring fear's false noises and turning up love-filled whispers. This practice kept me healthy and strong. When I lapsed into worry while meeting the multitudinous unknowns of authoring, a deep breath fully exhaled would call me back. Focused resilient energy proved essential.

One bright day an inspired notion occurred. Utilizing the blank side of five hundred pages of Providence St. Joseph's hospital records for a printed copy the book's manuscript. A whole new dimension of re-creation showed itself.

Shortly after I committed to book writing, Joseph and I enjoyed a lively phone conversation including personal theories about practical mysticism. I healed while I coalesced years of notes that helped shape this book. Levity training alongside visionary practice caused us both to lovingly laugh out loud.

Grace and Ease...

By late winter, the 1939 house felt too large. I loved its high-ceilinged curves and cozy coves. A small family would fill it better. Once I signed up with Westside rentals, initiating a new home search, common sense clicked in. I amended my 'vision home's specifics on a wish list: wouldn't it be nice if Diana of Trotta Realty had another small house? Imagining it would simplify a move in the midst of my writing project, I released my vision to the Universe.

In my ideal-home description, I'd envisioned a place near enough the foothills for hikes. An Earth-bound spot with abundant plants and trees. Diana's reply to my inquiry called for patience. "I may have something in a few months," she said. I was happy to wait. Trusting process had become more natural. By early spring, her tenants gave notice.

A morning walk enfolded a "go-look-see" at potential new abode. Six blocks away, old growth trees lined both sides of a small avenue. A charming little 1929 Spanish U-shaped home with a detached garage invited a closer look. My peeks through the windows hinted that these insides might be my next creative dwelling. In the backyard, an eighty-year-old avocado tree was pregnant and delivering.

"Yes," I replied to Diana, "let me know when it's a reality." Extensive clean up from the last tenants and interior work was required. My request for hardwood flooring was granted. Partial uncarpeted living space suited home yoga practices. Ease of lease transfer followed newly installed floorings, light fixtures and more. Life continued to bless and reflect balance in my steps.

My relationship with and need for entertainment had radically shifted. I used to be a movie-a-night addict. I ceased believing that I needed to be entertained. The big television I'd dragged along from the sold condo was given away—easily. One Craigslist "moving sale" ad brought people from multiple zip codes. A DVD and VHS collection were purchased by a dealer. Half a household of goodies and dusted-off storage items sold, with garage sale signs having gone up the night before. From daybreak on, the sale turned into a way to connect with others. One person's de-cluttering became another's delight.

In honor of Gwen Cochran's philanthropic last request, a portion of proceeds were tithed to a local temporary aid center. Gwen, a recently deceased eighty-plus, wiry yoga classmate from the YMCA, had inspired us all. Thank you, Gwen, for reminding me there are many ways to contribute. Tithing became a way of life. Here and in Mexico, my home communities benefit as I prosper and grow.

Today, I treat money and food with respect and trust. I didn't always. Lingering attachments melted on their own as resonant choice felt better. Borrowed library DVDs, or a keeper from my personal collection, played in my laptop occasionally. Recognizing movies as a reflection of my love of storytelling, I declined tyrannically eliminating this pastime all together. Yet a new energy rested within. Discernment thrived, supporting conscious choices of films and other leisure activities. Symbolic insights appeared in nature as telling directives. Intuition guided, and continues to guide, daily. Waking meditation—moment-to-moment living awareness—becomes increasingly available. Something wonderfully creative-mysterious occurs each day.

Committed to being with all manner of hypersensitivity, I purposely went to "scary places." And related with people in less than comfortable environs (for me), like Target, with a renewed perspective. I initiated friendly exchanges in Trader Joe's lengthy check out line. It was part of a conscious decision to dynamically interact with all people—unconditionally. Linda had imparted a simple clue at our monthly meditation circle: an authentic smile is an expression of love. We needn't say a thing. Simply remember often that we are the Light and see it in all other beings. Offering a quiet "God bless you" to frantic L.A. drivers became my private pleasure. Daily, I appreciate folk's apparent hurriedness as a reminder to be patient with myself and others.

My late April 2011 move could be summarized in three words: calmness in motion. Maureen Lee, a dear friend, etched time out of her busy schedule and lined wooden drawers and shelves while I coordinated with movers. While other friends and family sent 'moving' condolences, I experienced a constant flow of supportive synchronicities. They blew the lid off theories that moves must be stressful and difficult. The art of *being with what is* had become a friend.

The back end of the property duplex is home to friendly neighbors: Gabbie, a professional pet sitter and constant gardener of the backyard's flower-filled landscape, and Ed, a storyboard artist and writer who abides in the unit above hers. Jack and Jacque, Gabbie's cats, allowed me to make friends with them as well.

June 2011 marked a joyful birthday month, my 55th. An intended housewarming and early June birthday celebration was called off—honoring the newly embraced writing project. It became a focused priority. Friends responded with curious concerns, noticing me take a break from my "house warming/b-day" tradition. We created intimate "bite to eat" celebrations instead.

A Writer's Haven

Ralph Waldo Emerson quotes grace a rust-stained, concrete wall across the street from where I am living at the time of this writing. His namesake's elementary school playground is fifteen feet or so above sidewalk level. Children's playtime voices remind me to enjoy recess breaks as I write. Sometimes I sit in silence. Depending on Spirit's cue, I might be inclined to breathe through a few sets of Cat-Cow yogic spinal flexes, or reverse flow by swinging my legs up the wall of my home office. Or practice the Lama's heart-pumping "walk in place" exercise—always breathing deeply, sometimes dancing, singing off key and laughing.

Neighborhood dogs love the deep lush front lawn here. Some evenings I greet them and their owners outside for some fresh air. We share neighborly chats as pooches sniff and scratch. The lawn *used to be* an unattended poop pit. Dog owners are now invited to allow their canine's enjoyment, and thanked for being responsible and courteous with bagging up the residue. Green blades of grass (heart-chakra's resonant color hue) reflected my open mind's joyful sense of connection and clarity, nature's blanket for conversational moments— dogs and humans serendipitously satisfied.

Recently, one youthful dog-walker named Freddie paused, two leashed pups in tow. This young gentleman asked permission to offer a gift. Pointing out my front picture-window's hummingbird feeder, he mentioned its contents were less than the most desirable. His knowledge of the feeding habits of one of my lifetime totems educated me. We exchanged our shared appreciation for hummingbirds. To date, every four or so days, unseen by me, he manages to refresh the sweet liquid. A particular winged visitor has claimed the little red and yellow dome. Freddie said one would. Near twilight I may sit and watch. The rapid figure-eight movements of its wings carve the warm evening air. It balances mid-air to sip sweet nectar. I am graced by and with its Joy-filled presence while I look through the window at Life.

A life-vision mobile, which little Antoinette and I began creating at my old home hangs, in plain view. A flat vision board seemed too one dimensional, as I lovingly embraced my multi-dimensional Self. My inner child had nudged me to reconnect with my arts and crafts basket before the move. Symbols of my life's dynamic vision dangle from transparent fishing lines. Breezes drift through two-inch Venetian blind gaps. At times, they prompt the spontaneous dance of its wind chimes. A foam hummingbird floats over a silk flower bunch, mimicking the live ones all around the neighborhood. I'm glad I put the vital pieces of my life back together and dream about possibilities yet to appear. The mobile invites me to contemplate, meditate on what I like about life. And let it be. There is a bee on it, too, as a reminder of that.

Yes, there's a bee. A bright-smiled, wide-eyed, seven-inch-tall foam bee. Its flexible arms and legs reach out and up and down in an open-hearted posture. It was a novelty gift stuck inside a potted plant from Maureen. I glued a little rally sign on a long skinny stick and its miniature declaration pokes out from the bee's see-through wings, pieced together from magazine messages. They encourage me. "Let your Life be." "Give voice to your heart." These sayings inspire me, each time I walk past them. I enjoy symbols of self-encouragement, as well as honoring inner child's delight with glue and scissor play.

A miniature book dangles, too. A mini purple-and-green notebook from a Michaels' Arts and Crafts dollar bin rests inside a clear plastic alcove. "It" is the title. A golden-haired rain forest monkey is pictured on the reverse side. Its forward-facing, global eyes stare into the photographer's lens. Glue-pasted words—"See," "Inside," "Now," "Act"—surround its unique primate form. Wild mind rests behind the book's swaying motions.

Being here now, feels good. Doing what comes naturally. Giving and receiving are healthy habits. Heartfelt breaths support dimming down troublemaking gremlin tricks. Breath to breath—it is the way to live. I am empowered to envision soulful scenarios as I go where Spirit leads, merging with the consciousness movement on our planet as an expression of Being in my own unique way.

Joseph Campbell gave us a nudge to follow our bliss. It is what Life offers us as well. When we *do* from *who we are*, ordinary life becomes extraordinary existence.

Joy Now

Oh, what I had been missing out on for most of my adult life! Along my way I have yet to be in a conscious intimate partnership. While doing my ongoing inner work, clearing tears from fears, I reviewed a favorite recovery flick: *28 Days*. Sandra Bullock's character in rehab reflected a damaged ability to form and nourish intimate relationships. I like receiving clues from simple, everyday access points like movies. To make the long film's story short: a therapist told rehabbers if they could keep a plant alive for a year, they might move on and begin relating with a pet. The rehab counselor recommended they live with a living being before contemplating a healthy relationship. Sound therapeutic advice that flitted across my mind early autumn 2011.

I intended to treat myself to cut flowers at Trader Joe's check out. Potted plants were a step outside the electronic door. I paused while the cashier patiently gave me a moment to make up my mind. Okay, let's invite a plant into the house. It was one thing to enjoy the yard's flourishing Gabbie-green-thumbed blooms—and quite another to honor a live one myself. "Oh yes," I self-encouraged, "you can keep this sturdy Gerber plant flowering. Especially, if I'm careful about not over-watering it, as I learned from previously drowned adoptees. Keep it alive for a year, and maybe a little dog will come into your life."

I had never experienced relating with or caring about a pet. I had coveted my space, cleanliness and quiet. Being a sometime friend with Gabbie's cats stirred up memories of an attempt at pet adoption after my physical recovery had stabilized. Feisty was an outdoor cat who in a matter of days I returned to his foster mom. He was unhappy confined in the condo's non-escape route environment. I was not ready for feline predilections in my home.

At a Sunday Kundalini class held at Tanya and Eric's homegrown L.A. Yoga Garage, I chatted with Dorit, a photographer who had recently filmed animal shelter inhabitants. She had posted abandoned cats on her Facebook page and website. Dorit adopted one following great emotional losses, deaths and her recent divorce, all within a year. She shared what having PJ meant to her. Speaking in the language of energy balance, she attributed his presence to her healing through deep sadness and grief.

Dorit advocated I reconsider what a live being may bring to my current creative development challenges. I was hesitant, having just ventured into plant adoption, feeling nervous as I was very pregnant with the making of this book. During post-class teatime on Tanya's patio, I viewed Dorit's iPhone images. She wanted me to see a little calico tortie tagged as Peek-A-Boo by South Los Angeles' Animal Rescue shelter staff. I sighed an *"Oh My."* Feeling an open flow of inner guidance after yoga, I received an instantaneous message. *Keep an eye on that know-it-all stubbornness that no longer serves you.* I felt butterflies in my stomach.

Peek-a-Boo was soon to be anesthetized into forever, if not adopted pronto. I met her shivering self in a cage, staring out with huge yellowish green orbs. "Yes, please let me meet her," I offered the volunteer. She placed the six-month-old kitten in a "do not touch the animals" meeting area and waited patiently while the cat and I made eye contact. She feline-sneezed and heaved with a breathing difficulty I remembered experiencing myself a little while ago. Self-talk aided me in letting go of judgment saying, "Kiddo, wait and listen to what the med staff says." I heard all the logic and reasoning that told me, "No way, you can't care for a pet, not now!"

"How could I learn to care for this mysterious creature and stay focused with my creative project?" I wondered.

My knee-jerk reaction, in matters of committed relationships, had ranged from indecisive hesitating to feeling overwhelmed. I checked in with an old friend who cares for two cats, wanting some insights before deciding what to do. Sunday was my day of repose, yet time was of the essence for this little being. A call to Julia Lendl-Celotto, whom you'll meet further in Stage Seven, resounded what I felt in my heart.

"Yes, Antoinette," she said over her cell while tending to her Hawaiian Island garden plot. "It is a positive step toward inviting and relearning an exchange of genuine love. Gentleness with another living being is puuurfect for you, right now." She knew my relationship history, and I'd shared with her the conscious partnering desires stirring in my heart.

Julia's words flipped a switched and spoke deeply to my soul. Another spontaneous release occurred. A lingering hairball of resentment flew up and out, followed by a moment of tear wracking hidden sorrow. My mind opened as my heart melted away memories of being a little girl with adult responsibilities who had never learned the art of healthy relationship. I had grown up emotionally enslaved by co-dependent tendencies—with an addiction to control and a need to fix what I thought was broken in another and myself. I had consciously addressed these issues, and now I saw that there was a next step. In that miraculous moment, a chokehold of fear departed my entire being and I took a leap of trust.

Driving south on the 110 Harbor Freeway, I passed by my alma mater, USC, to meet Peek-a-Boo and begin experiencing life lessons

I'd avoided for too long. Peek-a-Boo has since been rechristened to Peeka, a name that suits her gorgeous nature. Right now, she lies curled up on my bed's cozy garnet fleece blanket, healing rapidly with minor medical care and much love. This healing feline teacher has been showing me, reminding me of a deeper meaning of love that *just is* within the simple day-to-day rhythms of life. Without a need to know or be in control of what comes next, I am still a little shocked that I adopted her. Yet, enjoying the enormous relief I feel from surrendering willful characteristics.

The renewal I'd experienced over the past few months unleashed joyful creative energy, moments of companionship, playful periods and quiet times. A simple act of non-resistance to the synchronistic connecting of dots shifted my perspective and brought another living being into my world. Daily life has a love connection I had no idea existed. I'd been an adamant dog lover, claiming I could never live with a cat in the house. She blessed my life the moment I met her, helping me relax and become curious as a cat looking at everything anew.

Before I met Peeka, I'd gone with Dorit to meet PJ and get a little more information. We were walking down the street from Tanya and Eric's Yoga Garage to her Highland Park bungalow when Dorit had commented on my parked Matrix's JOY NOW California license plate. *"I like that,"* she had offered. As I stepped off the curb to cross the midline of their quiet residential street, I'd smile in agreement. *"I like it, too."*

I would soon experience anew, my intentional personalized plate. Falling in love when I spent moments looking into the universe of Peeka's eyes was an everyday miracle previously unbeknownst to me. She has helped deepen my love and ability to interact with others, in a calm respectfully loving way.

I am endlessly fascinated, being led by my Heart in the continuum of Life.

Sixth Stage Life Process

Stage Six energy governs our mental capacities. The openness of our sixth chakra connects us with intuitive mind's wisdom and understanding.

The sixth chakra is located in the middle of our forehead, a spot that sacred Eastern traditions refer to as our "third eye." Sixth-charka energy regulates our brain and neurological system, including the pituitary and pineal glands, as well as the functioning of our nose, eyes and ears.

Stage Six energy governs the mind or "mental body." Synonymous with our psychological makeup, our mental body represents accumulated wisdom accessed throughout our life. This includes all we know, from actual facts (ideas that members of society agree to be true) as well as concepts we've adopted as truth. The mental body encompasses our fears, learned experiential knowledge and how we interpret incoming data.

Going further, Stage Six energy is not only the regulatory center for our intellectual capabilities but our emotional intelligence as well. An improved state of emotional intelligence will shine forth in our ability to discern what is appropriate advice or guidance. In this stage, we ready ourselves to become the individual creative expression of who we are in our spiritual essence.

When the Third Eye Opens...

The observable levels of wisdom range from habitual unconscious thought patterns, emotional intelligence and creative visualization capabilities onward to extrasensory perception. Higher inspiration and insights are reached when this chakra opens. Visionary perceptions arrive with expanded higher consciousness.

When sixth chakra's third eye begins to open, we become truth seekers. We are deeply committed to discovering unique qualities of our spirit, and let them shine through our personal contributions to the lives of others. At this level of maturity, we decline illusory concepts, being seekers of a higher symbolic truth within each present moment.

At this stage's development, our challenge is to learn the art of Presence. Guided by the higher level of our intuitive mind, we become present to our thoughts and their related emotional-energetic impulses. Our conscious presence empowers us to make choices from a purposeful perspective. The energy of this stage fortifies our ability to make conscious choices arrived at through cooperation with intuitive insight. We learn to look for, see and hear higher perspectives.

This sixth wheel of energy contributes added equilibrium to our Stage Five co-creative expressions. It demonstrates the universal truth that form materializes from our mental energy, which comprises thought-emotion frequencies. In this divine play, these currents of energy appear to project forth from our heart-minds, into the realm of infinite potentiality, to create physical manifestations.

As we embrace the wisdom of Stage Six, we honor the universal truth that all creation is initiated in the energy dimension. And that our mental-emotional energy is a precursor of manifestation. We recognize that it truly is a re-creational universe. Our appreciation of Its Nature, co-joined with our higher perspectives, gives us an ability to play.

Our variable perception is representative of sixth chakra energy. When this chakra is open and unblocked, we see greater truths than previously experienced. We learn to give Life our full attention as higher Intelligence sense-feelings arise from a higher perspective. Experiencing heart-mind-body integration, we consciously realign with higher truth as a Self-nurturing energy choice. We make a practice of consciously raising our mental-energy frequency vibration with the insights we receive from higher mind, all the while remaining receptive to further shifts of thought processes.

Stage Six's openness inspires us to bring our best, focused mental-emotional energy to every circumstance. We honor being fully present as an act of great love that intentionally creates thriving relationship with all aspects of life. The secret to play is our openness to this stage's insights, as we cultivate an ability to follow higher mind's intuitive guidance and imagination rather that our uniformed reasonable, rational intellect. We eventually become a capable visionary, freed up to co-create our most beautiful life experiences.

Our mental-emotional energy body's relative health determines the ease with which we meet this stage's process. It is where our mind walks the bridge between our psyche and transcendent Self. Higher Self and our psyche together represent the dominant nature of our mental-emotional energy, which in turn reflects the active level of wisdom we posses. In the words of the Indian sage Sri Ramakrishna: "It is our mind that makes us wise or ignorant— bound or emancipated."

Being Big in Mind

Zen teachings distinguish Big mind from small mind. The lessons Stage Six offers activate our Big mind. Incorporating with the wisdom we gained through life experience, Big mind identifies with life's process and is open minded. Its symbolic sight is capable of being impersonal and experiences life with a detached presence. Thus in Stage Six's opening we develop conscious non-attachment by embodying the higher truth we perceive. Knowing no outer entity affects changes in our lives, we are solely responsible when unified with the divine dynamic of life.

Big mind operates from a universal perspective. As it participates in a field of infinite possibilities, it remains open to solutions that spontaneously appear "out of the blue." Big mind participates with life from the energy of forgiveness, acceptance, insight, attention and connectedness. It regards deeper meanings of life with reverence.

Small mind is underdeveloped, lower-level egoic energy. It thinks only of itself, and reacts in compulsive, limited mechanical fashion. Small mind feeds on itself, from its fear-based mentality. Its fear reacts to fear, judgment reacts to judgment, and anger sparks more anger.

When ego's small mind is lost, limitation is lost. We become infinitely kind and Big-minded in consciousness. This is the spiritual power available to us in the Sixth Life Process of transformation. Our Big mind is our visionary psyche. At its fully developed state, it becomes our visionary response with all of life. Thinking from Big mind, we become capable of discerning what is right action, and what is real achievement.

Process as a Way of Life

An open third eye perceives process as a way of life. Process includes our ability to return inside and review, evaluate and excavate lingering unconscious holding patterns that block full-bodied chakra energy flow. Any and every thought form hidden in the recesses of small mind is calmly observed. Our impersonal, neutral attention creates space, allowing us to witness the delusional aspects of small mind's content. Unifying open third eye wisdom with our heart power, we readdress our psychological fears. Seventh chakra's transcendental spiritual nature connects us with the power of Higher Consciousness.

When this stage's process commences, fear of change is a lurking energy challenge. We witness it with our conscious disciplines. We seek higher truth and listen for Higher Self guidance. We are better able to work through revisits with our mental-emotional de-cluttering process. Our ability to reevaluate illusive aspects of our psychological patterns is strengthened by this stage's energy. When our open third eye functions in tandem with our heart center, we are empowered to metaphorically see and hear "into ourselves" more clearly and to greater depths.

Our commitment to conscious awareness stimulates sixth chakra energy. Third eye focused awareness in unison with our breath bridges our mind with the wisdom of our Heart center. The third eye and heart chakra are oft chosen points of focus during meditation and other conscious breathing practices. We can invite such awareness practices into our present moment, anywhere and anytime: conscious breath to conscious breath, deliberately being present.

Our Higher Self has the power to release us from psychological states of mental dysfunction. Third eye wisdom supports our liberation from mental pictures—which in this stage we realize are emotionally charged holograms of fear-based thinking. Guided by Higher Self we are empowered to break the habit of permitting negative self-validation as a source of aliveness. Its wisdom relieves us of being a constant complainer of situations, living from a victim-perpetrator mentality.

Instead, we are guided to inspired use of our intellect's capabilities. Wise discernment brings clarity as we honor the inherent value of increased symbolic insights and inspirational messages. As our wisdom expands, we are able to self-evaluate in an absence of judgment or criticism. Our truth-seeking missions are regarded as our being an instrument in service of Universal Mind. Choice discernment improves as confusion lessens. When we open to this stage of consciousness, we readily see the humorousness of our human foibles.

Meeting Our Shadow

Once we are brought to clarity and higher wisdom, we are still susceptible to "red herring" episodes. Our false self prompts all manner of fear-based thinking. Our increased awareness senses toxic thoughts ideas-false concepts, or actions—most likely the same ones we worked through and gained ground on releasing. The thoughts we declared "no longer held authority over us" are viewed as shadow aspects of our personality.

When we meet the shadow side of our personality with openness, we are supported. Our Big mind works in tandem with unseen forces, as we surrender to further self-administered psychological review. We are empowered to observe and examine lingering negative habits of thought, dispassionately. Reframing, and subsequently turning around, old programming begins by first making peace with where we are, willing to move on. This is the power of watching and noticing the trail of thought-emotions that drift through our active thought processes. Our conscious connection with Source alchemizes lower, fear-based thinking into higher perspectives of love-originated thoughts.

We now know greater outcomes are possible while we simultaneously understand that we are not in control of the process. We are co-operating with Source. At this stage, we develop a wise sense of reality, recognizing our intentional attention and vision for outcomes is solely our responsibility. We relinquish a need to control anyone or anything, other than our conscious choices. Wisely understanding the uselessness of a chronic human behavior, we choose to let go of attempts to control. We loosen the hold that fear, doubt and worry had on our mind, and we surrender to insightful choice.

Our commitment to remain present connects us with Higher Mind in every context and in all experiences. This commitment is the worthiest of our spiritual practices. It is the living, breathing resurrection of our essential human Being. A peaceful, inspired disposition is a quality of an open third eye and adopted in our daily living. Akin to a quiet watcher's composure on the bank of a passing stream, we watch life go along its natural course. Our detached demeanor is a willingness to go with Life's flow. We are readied to rise and do our part when the next step shows itself.

Our patient presence practices fulfill this stage's ongoing Conscious Discipline. It empowers us to wait, watch and listen for what is next. Life energy is now perceived as a continuum. Acceptance of the temporary nature of all things, in tandem with an appreciation of the nature of life, is demonstrated with surrendered grace and ease.

Life After (Fear of) Death

Our spiritual maturity avails us a freedom from fear of bodily death. We willingly reckon with ego death, recognizing ourselves as immortal energy being. Observing the ego mind's shenanigans from a detached place of love, we are freed to truly be alive. In unison with seventh chakra's quality of higher knowledge, we realize continuity of life as the energy that currently shapes our human form. Energy never dies. We are never "done" evolving, yet we are consciously focused to *be here now*.

Our realization of eternalness invites unlimited perception and allowance of Consciousness. Inner truths may feel unnamable, our experiences untranslatable by social our cultural norms. We may discover a relaxed demeanor regarding a need for any particular religion or philosophical school of thought. Reflecting the ineffable quality of our spiritually evolved Nature, we respect the vast variety of wisdom paths Infinite Intelligence created.

With sixth chakra energy open, we gain the ability to do effortlessly what we previously did with effort. Revisits with introspective practices, contemplative studies and meditative states are woven into our lifestyle. We legitimize all prior inner work by reviewing lingering secondary aspects of ourselves. We are able to self-inquire: *what do I believe, why do I believe this?* We invite breakthroughs via our conscious inner inquiries, and demonstrate willingness to wait for Greater answers. We master "thought watching" to such a degree that our answers to both above questions may arrive unanticipated.

We watch our responses to life and sense truth received from our Higher Self. Often insight flashes into our conscious awareness in the course of the day. While out and about in the world, we may be given symbolic hints and clues to the answer we were seeking. Our open mind notices details and messages previously overlooked. This trustworthy process clears our mind, yielding increased cerebral benefits.

The evolved intellect bows to the imagination's insightfulness and watches visionary ideals unfold. Our symbolic sight becomes ever more strengthened by taking ownership of its realness. It gives us a "sixth sense" empowered by Divine reason. We trust so-called irrational or unreasonable choices, when prompted by Inner Being.

Opened sixth stage reflects our conscious awareness to tune into greater levels of possibilities. Unconscious concepts of "accidental connections" and "coincidences" become perceived as beneficial synchronicities in our day-to-day existence. Spontaneous synchronicities are welcomed as an understandable part of our reality.

There may be a natural passage of "commitment oscillation," as family or friends may have a different perspective on Life. We may feel wary at the possibility of losing long-held relationships by moving further into union with Source. We often choose to spend time in quiet solitude, willingly in retreat, wanting the solace of alone time. We honor the power of allowing change, trusting we are in a consciousness expanding process.

Those dearest to us will be there when we return—and our higher consciousness will magnetize like-heart-minded companions our way. We invite and accept an invitation to a broader connection with community. It is an aspect of our spiritual emergence to connect with others, with whom we share a resonant wavelength. This is a natural course of change that occurs as third eye openness further evolves us.

Self acceptance empowers us to release the need to fit into societal definitions, surrendering concern for how we seemingly appear to others. Our efforts give us an insightfulness that allows us to feel confident, when those around us may be feeling anxious. We exude peace and lightness of being as we reclaim our divine right to be our true Self. Our very presence may lift others' spirits without any effort on our part.

We choose aspirations of intentional contribution at this level of consciousness. It is, in truth, a joyful arrival—a worthy quest of shifted awareness has occurred. Now broken free of the chains of false self, we are given greater access to living from enlightened awareness. We resonate with Source-inspired energy, living in a state of grace and ease.

Sixth Self-Inquiry

Here is another opportune moment to relax
into your breathing....Have as many moments
as you like to settle in comfortably.

Ready to begin?

~ What are my deepest fears of living a consciously aware life? What
do I believe will occur if I embody soulful Presence? What do I
believe I might lose? How might I benefit?

~ What habitual thoughts do I have that limit my personal interactions?
What beliefs obstruct my relationships with others? How often do
I hear negative interpretations of experiences playing out in my
mind?

~ What attitudes and habits of thought leave me feeling disempowered? What beliefs stymie my resonant alignment with higher perspectives?

~ Would I describe myself as judgmental? What situations or interpersonal relationships trigger a judgmental tendency?

~ Am I willing to release being judgmental? If not, what pattern of belief is blocking my ability to be non-judgmental?

~ Am I currently relating with Life from an impersonal, open minded response? If not, what beliefs are my attitudes based on? What are they providing insights into?

~ What inordinately profound truths have I perceived, yet I continue to disbelieve or doubt? How might I allow them to be more accessible and resonant?

~ Have I experienced intuitive insights that surprised or startled me? If so, what choices have I made when they occur?

~ Am I willing to follow my inner wisdom in the face of no agreement? How might my life benefit when I ready myself and commit?

~ What disempowering excuses do I recognize that hold me back or leave me feeling stuck? How often do I make excuses that delay allowance of changes I want to make?

Now is an opportune moment to access change with Micro Moves. And a reminder of Heart-Mind questions in Self-Care Selections.

ONE PRESENCE

All

We did

We did

To

Be

Here

Now

AML

Seventh Inspiration

"Fundamental reality is pure potentiality. Our version is the
possibilities we choose."
—Deepak Chopra

It is all here. I see it in its Wholeness. It's all here when I let it be freed
up from the vice grips of resistance. Wired to a rat-tail, it dropped
down Alice's rabbit hole. A subtle whinny sound echoes, *"I'm late,
I'm late for a very important date"*... and control's devices drown.

I saw myself in the rush and worry of others and knew it was
an aspect of myself. An aspect that had been *waiting* with infinite
patience to be loved---expanded into existing perceptibly as its
true essence. Alchemized fear released Source energy, renewing by
capacity to perceive the Wholeness of me.

A knowing bubbled up from my depths that *I never do anything
wrong—and I never have to get anything right*. That I Am free to
simply Be.

The dynamic nature of life's process unravels seeming opposites.
All that is left is a feeling experience. Just when it seems we are on
the verge of drowning in an ocean of emotional choice, ascending

currents invite us to rise above hellish fear…into warm welcoming waters of celestial love.

From our human perspective, the vast and endless cosmos that connects us is earthbound space and time—a simultaneously safe, scary and sacred construct we experiment within. This playground of illusion offers us all we will ever need to expand and grow beyond space and time without leaving bodily form. It is our co-creative life's field wherein we watch dots connect one to another like chains of DNA morphing into full-sized living, breathing, walking, talking beings. Energy fleshed out is our land of evolving opportunity.

Freedom to be free blinks in, blinks out. Light flashes hint at us from the corner of our peripheral vision. Neighboring dimensions drift like waves of transparency, nanosecond vapors return to invisible—gone, poof! It is all made up, so what's to resist except nothing at all. Dip into the primordial ooze and find all concepts gone, but One. That Life is here to be enjoyed with an energy so palpable we taste its sweet powerful peace and know it as our Essence.

Oh, that's what I came here for. To meet my inner Maker, to be a unified expression of unknowable, inconceivable Energy, beyond human comprehension. Simply to be felt, sensed, sipped, breathed, bathed and basked in. Danced with time and time again. Worlds without end. Amen. Realized ineffable spirits dancing in space timelessly at play, the space where I is We and there is no place else to be but Here and Now.

Experimenting on the edge of moments, we return to the spaciousness we came from. Gone another moment over another disappears without a trace. I am me. You are you. We are we. Endless beings of inseparable energy dance.

Free to choose, blink in and out—light flashes off and on. Limitations dissolve in the wink of an eye. Attention laser-beamed through vaporous fog, Love's Light guides us on. Enjoy the never-ending cosmic, comedic, profound, poignant, experiential energy Dance of Life. Moment to moment, a rich evolutionary revolution beckons: *"Come, come to the edge."* But we're afraid. *"Come,"* It calls us. We step forth. It breathes us. And we fly . . .

Heart to Heart

It is nearly Thanksgiving 2011, in the U.S.A. Greetings to my Canadian friends and vacation rental guests were sent last month. Walgreen's flu shot signs are on display, front and center. Dr. Lee asks each year if I will take one and accepts that I continue to decline. As winter approaches, my three-month check up appointment does, too, and I'll decline once more if he asks. Summer's blood tests resulted in Dr. Lee's calmly hinting at lupus remission. His words: "I hesitate to use the 'r' word just yet, but your tests keep pointing in that direction." I replied, "You mean retired?" We chuckled with our smiles.

Physical cautionary signals, courtesy of stroke and lupus history, were energy companions during the co-creation of this book, however infrequently they showed up. The mildest of bodily sensations, ignored in 2006, were treated as wisdom messages. Heart-listening had vastly expanded. Knee joints, symbolic of our flexible capacity to move onward in life, occasionally sent prickly sensations when I pushed myself too hard. "Easy does it," my Higher Self guided. "Calm down . . .s l o w down . . . breathe deeply into your belly. Exhale fully."

Deeper understanding of each chakra center's evolving process and the causative factors that led to near death invited daily reflections. Source conducted day-to-day revisions of my interpretation of living in a state of grace. Resonant energy alignments guided me on.

Pre-planned, well thought-out "how to" productivity systems collapsed. Each day, though the day before may have been an existential wonderment, ongoing inner outer shifts and changes called me back to be reverently present. Divine directions continuously reset the pace and the plan.

Late summer 2011 proved a roller coaster ride—up, down, heaven, hell. Fiery visits with the depth of my soul had undone me again. I knew myself since age six as a spiritual being. Back then it expressed as a desire to serve God through martyrdom or becoming a cloistered nun, before the advent of boys in adolescence shifted my nunnery aspirations. So there I sat, in the warmth of summer, an evolving adult. Returned from the breech of human existence four years hence and invited to live purposefully, I felt a deeper shift underway, again.

Alive and well, up to goodness and service...and still resistant fear returned in earnest. I sought solace journaling with God and reopening bedside books. I reread Mirabai Starr's contemporary translations of the *Dark Night of the Soul*. Again I was, undergoing rapid changes, personality disassembled, "identity-less-ness" being assimilated into life by my soul.

Dark night of Spirit had called. It was another aspect of transcendence, a final passage, not always entered, or so I understood from St. John of the Cross' *Dark Night* immersion. Yet as a hint of a higher invitation arose—struggle had reared its resistant head.

Starr's work calmed me. I felt worthy when I remembered that I had remembered who I am—yet humbled as I released and forgave inner critic's comments about my windy road of vocational detours. There was a moment when I heard questions about the creation of this book, when so many already exist with a similar message. But I recognized the saboteur fright behind the questioning. I had answered a genuine calling, so no matter what I went on with my divine errand. Heart center became a safe haven to check in, listen and release doubt. Great Mother energy was and continues to be embraced in the womb-like folds of my burgundy fleece blanket. I surrendered to Sacred feminine creative timing.

My scariest duo paradigm had haunted me: "fear of not knowing" and "fear of not getting it right." These false constructs, affronts to life's changeable nature, were ego entrapment that tried to co-opt my heart's power. Yet they could no longer pollute my energy or an inspired mission's unfolding. Now I had tools, heart-empowering options for daily use. Noticing when tension claimed my neck or shoulders, I moved through it and exhaled released. "Ahhhhhh... There you are, you illusionary demon." A deep breath into my heart center exhaled waves of Light—and *poof!* Fearful aspect dissipated. Devotion to breath and movement cleared dark thought-storms, freeing me to relax and stand in my truth. I addressed, in deep appreciation of symbolic sight, bodily signals telegraphing a need to shift, to realign mind-body frequency with Source energy.

Peeka's cat stretches and naps came as a reminder of nature's play and rejoined me with my own. Cat Cow and Downward Facing Dog yoga asanas (postures) spontaneously combusted stored energy. Simultaneous spinal adjustments popped with increased regularity. Kitty mama duties gave the 'So what...' mantra a new appreciative meaning. Peeka trained away lingering rigidity about how things are supposed to happen. And my magical inner child joined in the fun of evening romps and playful games. Inner child's ageless knowing transmissions from eons of space and time experiences consistently wizened me up and empowered my heart.

A previously disruptive habit of self-confusion was met with grace. It became a sensing practice as elements of the book grew into wholeness. Color-coded inspired ideas, as well as a collection of materials from the last four years, were laid out in several rooms.

Thinking I'd misplaced a next micro-step item, I declined becoming confused. This was a nice newness of improvisational receptivity. I closed my eyes, purposely blind to any distractions from outer stimuli, and asked *where could it be?* A brief picture of the potential location of item appeared. Repeatedly the exact placement of the "lost" resource, communiqué or note was revealed in a nanosecond image on a screen inside my mind. Trust blossomed alongside reverence for endless inspiration and inflow of Inner direction in crafting of the book. Life also taught me to slow down and be more present so I would remember where I had put something in the first place.

When I remembered that this is my renewed way of life, I felt my way through each day. When I forgot, I pushed forward missing clues, going to bed tired and spent. Those nights served as a reminder that I enjoy even-energy expenditure. I also received spiritual guidance in sitting consultations and e-mail correspondences with Linda Neaman Lee, my friend from Pause Your Mind Meditation. Once the book's vision, collection of journals, notes, and hospital records invited structure, I had desired collaborative co-creative input.

Linda and I sat on Pause Your Mind meditation cushions asking that blessings of love be sent around the Earth. It was Sunday, September 11, 2011. Loving prayers were being expressed worldwide. Fear is only contagious when we believe it is real. So is Love. We felt it to be an auspicious fourth chakra energy day for our "look see" of the rough draft of my manuscript. Our task centered on sorting out and clarifying its intended heart-mind offering. We playfully brainstormed meaningful titles and subtitle ideas.

Linda's affirming spiritual direction re-grounded me, fortifying my intentions. We occasionally traveled our consult session to the upstairs level, invigorating our hearts and bodies. Both of us invited in new insights as Pacific Ocean's salty air drifted through the ground-level studio door. I was glad I had followed my heart to her Venice Beach doorstep. I felt centered and reconnected with inner dreams. The loosening of mental constraints lightened a pathway, illuminated by clarity of committed direction.

Aloha Mahalo

My dear friend Julia Lendl-Celotto, a Hawaiian transplant from Simi Valley, California, became this book's spiritual godmother, my reclaimed sister and a mystical playmate. She had been my best friend at USC, where we were Women's Track and Field teammates. Julia's former high jumper's lithe pro-volleyball moves now grace the sands of the big island of Hawaii. I had let our former friendship die a slow death not facing my inner competitive and resentful interpretations of our past. She waited for years, silently, for something to open. Around the time I was moving here, leaving the 1939 viola home, a light went on inside my heart.

"Aloha" is a sacred Hawaiian word, equal in profundity as Namaste. It welcomes another's divine presence in every greeting of breath shared. It represents allowance, nurturance of a sacred space for Divine awareness. The gorgeous light that went on inside my heart was my missed friendship with Julia, and a desire to call her with an Aloha wish. She sounded beyond joy when I phoned with congratulations for her dream-come-true relocation to Hawaii. It had been her lifelong vision made real at fifty years of age.

She expressed her disappointment at not knowing or being present when I experienced what I needed to go through to be here now. I assured her that, just like Joseph's e-mail vibrations, *"You were there—you just didn't know it. Mahalo, Julia."*

"Mahalo" is a sacred Hawaiian blessing of gratitude for All-That-Is—beyond space and time. *Prana*, breath, our life force, is inherent in the meaning of both of these words. I breathed a sigh of relief and delight at her absolute acceptance of my reconnecting.

We unsurprisingly discovered our paths had similar "wake up" stratagem designed within their framework. Loss and seeming tragedies had called forth her spiritual seeker's heart time and time again. We shared our embrace of human trials and tribulations as accepted passages of the evolution of our souls. And we realized our emotional-memory releases opened up higher energies that recreated our ways of living.

As I took in Linda's higher mind ministrations and collaborative offerings, Julia's spiritual-athlete energy encouraged and inspired my own. Sunday morning's island-to-mainland phone call 'meet-ups' began with a Natalie Goldberg style "writing practice" partnership. Julia, a mastered teacher of learning-challenged youth, had recently resumed a photography aspiration. Her images, adorned with quotes and original messages that match them, are sold in galleries and at local art fairs. Our practice sessions of read-listen, read-listen became a soulful sisterhood's field of infinite possibilities.

After my birthday this year, Julia sent a belated photographic b-day gift with one of my favorite quotes, now placed above the brick-faced fireplace to inspire book's unfolding. Clouds break and clear as Hawaiian sunrise opens space for Chuang Tzu's message of guidance:

> *"Easy is right. Begin right and you are easy.*
> *Continue easy and you are right.*
> *The right way to go easy...is to forget the right way...*
> *And forget that the going is easy."*

Easy flow of process was becoming the norm, yet occasionally I flinched from a bit of brain strain. Julia listened and offered a few practical advisements regarding gremlin saboteur's capers. "Antoinette, Two Ton's **not so** mean, soft trickster voice wasn't working. So it had to pull out all stops. It knows your soft points… and wants to halt you in your tracks."

Yes! Co-creative volley for Supreme Being's team! I had heard a few monkey-mind buzz words. Small mind was saying I was *supposed* to go it alone. That asking for help meant I was *not good enough, unworthy* of authorship. It was pitifully pissed off that I hadn't *quit* when it said I *should.* I joyfully exclaimed to Julia, dancing around the living room: Not one of us creates anything alone, none of us, ever!

Poof! Another delusional control construct bit the dust.

During a "tools of the trade" supply run to Office Depot, a rolled Rand McNally world map caught my attention. A view of our planet's landmasses and vast oceans now hangs on the living room wall, nearby the front window's hummingbird watch station. I look at our world, seeking out geographic locations of friends near and far. Warm tea mug in hand, I stand taking in a paper version of earth's magnificent beauty, wondrous waters and mountainous elevations blended into oneness. A clearance table's one-dimensional sale item reflects deeper higher truths of our planetary connectedness.

Julia's oldest son, Mario, Air Force TACP airman stationed in the remote mountains of Afghanistan, awaits returning to his stateside wife. Mario stands in full knowing that wars—political and religious aggressions that devalue Life—are not acts of Who We Really Are. It was the available job.

Julia's and my prayers envisioned peace and a worldwide contagion of belief in Love. A knowing wars will end when we all find our ways to alignment with Source. We visualized a new energy shifting our global community into a heaven-on-Earth experience, prompted by a global let-go of what no longer works.

Rabia Erduman's Afterword in *Veils of Separation* offers a predictive vision of our Aquarian Age: *"When enough of the conditioned responses to life have fallen away, two things remain: ecstasy and stillness...."* Oh, joyful quiet when peace and freedom are forever available. Hence, worldwide, *inside jobs* have been and must be personally attended to. Namaste. Aloha. Mahalo. All reflections of our universal language, Love.

Now is Forever

This book's vision and collaborative co-creation was an extraordinary invitation to deepen in the experiences of all stage's lessons and sacred truths. This process included seeing the realness of miraculous rebirth, an initiation I received on an August day in ICU. Universal messages from beyond me flowed as I listened to my Higher Self cues. Remembrance of ancient knowing and sacred practices invited allowance of seventh chakra energy. Each day, I return gladly to further-expanded training, fully aware of the practical mystic I am. Resounding blessings of joy and stillness deLight my human-grounded lightness of Being.

These days I wake early, loving the quiet of pre-dawn hours. Slow, deep, long breaths come first, quieting mind's stirring. Then wiggling of fingers and toes, rolling of wrists and ankles, stretching of legs and arms and breathing deeply into full-bodied twists. Life force stirs amongst flesh and bones, akin to the head-to-toe bodily awakening after *shavasana* (corpse pose) at end of yoga class. As my feet touch the ground, appreciation vibrates out in all directions. These and other impromptu morning practices welcome the day.

Later on, a shower's purifying waters wash away the past. I lotion and give thanks to my resilient body-temple for its divine carriage of my soulful heart. Then I smile into my eyes at the bathroom mirror with a silent "ready to Be...okay let's go Be..."

Source rests inside us all. *A Course in Miracles* sequence of Higher Self inquiry serves as a wisdom roadmap:

-Where would you have me go?
-What would you have me do?
-What would you have me say?
-And to whom? —

I enjoy this friendly exercise, available whenever a next step is unknown. These four inquiries effectively clear red herring's "turn left" when real direction is straight ahead. My spiritual understanding has vastly expanded since Catholic school days, leading to a shifted perspective of God. Deepak Chopra's *How to Know God* wisdom tome says as much for us all. We experience God as we experience our relationship with Life. I experience Life, God as nameless, unknowable Source Energy. It is always operating through everyone and everything. The Divine Mystery we call God may be more likened to a verb or function, an eternal evolutionary process in us and active around us infinitely. It is not to be contained as a word, concept or an image outside ourselves.

Where we join Source is within each conscious breath, with Source as its provider, benevolently empowering us to breathe in *"I Am as God created me—in Its likeness."* We are as God created us. Source energy, Its likeness. And we evolve day by day anchored in this eternal energy Truth, doing our psyche-Lamaze practices, breathing and choosing resonant expanded Connection moment to every loving moment.

Here we are Being human, actively aware of Its presence within every Divine atomic particle of form. We are God's children with same qualities of being. Absolute Truth. Absolute Oneness. Here to remember and be Life's Love. In all its contrast and assortment of infinite experiences, we choose our divine right to choose.

A metaphoric heaven rests behind our eyes and within our Heart as Spirit leads us to allow process. We look inside our Big mind with feet planted. We see truth, breathe, listen and do our inner work. Divine graces us through, supporting our transcendence of seeming obstacles.

Here we are. Maybe we deliver mail. Pick the kids up from school. Or drop them off...for their first year of college. Or make pizzas to pay the rent and night school tuition. Our hearts hum a tune of joy. We've done our work. We've accepted what life has placed at our feet, in our hands. It has taught us well as we remembered who we are. We walk our walk. We live our talk. We trust life, being trusting and trustworthy human Beings. We now live Truth. Right here, right now.

Life goes on. We used to chop wood, carry water and stir the fire. Here and now we catch planes, send Instagrams and check e-mail, even while walking down the street. Times have changed. We remain collective energy Beings. Co-creator Beings of Source energy. Eternal Oneness.

Seventh Stage Life Process

The Seventh Life Process represents our spiritual nature's evolution. Our seventh 'crown' chakra, the receptor of our non-physical vital energy *(prana)*, rests at the top of our head. This energy center exists as a depository of the divine grace we receive through kind thoughts and actions and internal awareness practices: prayer, meditation and all manner of consciously connecting with God/Universal Creator. The seventh chakra is our spirit-mind-body connection to the transcendent dimension of life.

In the ancient East Indian spiritual and healing system known as Ayurveda, *prana* is described as the vital "breath" energy of life, comparable to Chinese *qi* and Japanese *ki*. This life-sustaining energy flows in through our crown chakra and is focused in our brain. It is pure Source energy, the raw life force responsible for our heartbeat and breathing. Vital energy is especially concentrated along the midline of our central nervous system. *Prana* moves through and permeates our body's major systems. Nourishing our body, mind and spirit, seventh chakra energy flows throughout our muscular system and skin, and is distributed to our lower six chakra centers.

Open, balanced Stage Seven mind-emotion qualities—those of universal (cosmic) consciousness, transcendent ideas, inspirational and prophetic thought—are resultant of awareness practices of the highest order. Our commitment to meditation, inner awareness practices, inquiry, contemplative study, and prayer offerings sustains our mystical center's alignment with Source. When the crown chakra is open and receptive of divine energy, our life choices are made entirely from a Higher perspective. We perceive all aspects of our life as a unified field of divinity. God is seen/felt in every detail in us and around us.

Seventh Heaven via the "Dark Night of the Soul"

Our Stage Seven challenge is to "loosen the hold" that the material world has on our spirit, while we realign our implicit trust in Source with an absence of fear-interference. We turn our entire life over with unwavering trust. Our paramount fear, aroused when we receive an invitation to unify with God, shows up as a "dark night of the soul" experience.

This "dark night of the soul" is an often over-used terminology that diminishes its origination in St. John of The Cross's poetic narrative. Here we refer to it in its highest spiritual translation. It is not simply a passing phase or ordinary loss, but an extraordinary reversal of all former connections and identity with outer life as we once knew it. We arrive at sacred crossroads, feeling an absence of meaning in our life. We are at a loss, completely blind to our purposeful contribution to life. What we were accustomed to relying on as fulfilling no longer sustains satisfaction. Oftentimes dark nights are experienced as passages of time in between the familiar and the yet to be shown— ironically, we often enter them by way of an inner awakening that invites us to the make friends with the unknown. And in the midst of them, we lose our sense of outer identity while feeling confused as to what is our intended life purpose.

Nothing that used to comfort us provides solace. Our dark night crisis sends us into a deeper state of devotional practice. We pray for grace to show us a way out of the darkness. We are fearful that we have been abandoned by God, left to suffer for lapses in faithfulness. Yet we never lose faith or trust as we journey into the depths of our soul. We hope and trust that our good-feeling resonant Connection will return and guide us to a renewed life, and discovery of its deeper meaning and purposefulness.

The Call to Oneness

Seventh Life Process, calls us to be consciously present, surrendering all past-future fear-based thought patterns that we consciously realize no longer serve our alignment with Source. Our aspiration is to be actively present. Live with Inner Awareness as our guide to our highest truth, moment to moment. It is the greatest challenge of human life—when the seventh chakra opens and calls us to ascend and be one with Source energy while living grounded in our human form. Our devotional practices preserve our Connection as we wait out the shifts that are shaking us to our core. When no outer power can quell our fears, we instead turn to a Divine presence within.

Seventh Stage process work, not unlike our fourth chakra's inner child reclamation, often is better assimilated in the company of professional counsel. It requires we return to previous stages, allowing Grace to clear unconscious thought-emotion patterns. This may include reexamining our mind's old narratives, shadow issues and sticky mind habits that still have a hold on our psyche. At this time, it is necessary to create a reliable support system that grounds this momentous transition. Respect for crossing to the other shore—from the material realm of the outer world to a transcendental mystical paradigm of a vast Infinite dimension, while maintaining connection with human life—requires our attentiveness and self-nurturing habits' support. It is a formidable spiritual undertaking that requires absolute tending of self-care.

During this stage, helpful practices include: self-created release rituals, deep crying releases, connecting with Great Mother-earth energy, and spending time in sunshine (sun is also symbolic of *prana*). As we balance our daily meditation, prayer and inner awareness practices, we deepen in self-knowledge and inner knowing. Spiritual wisdom expands.

Mindfully witnessing the balance (or imbalance) resultant of our perseverance returns us to our Heart center, again and again. Remaining humble and reverent to the process, we willingly stay on path knowing all eventualities will appear in Natural timing.

When we've gone through dark night passages, we recognize our responsibility is to remain consistent—not obsessive—in our alignment with Source. Our courage to remain conscious, living beyond illusion and delusion fuels our passion to live as our Authentic Self. It is also our challenge to Be our Authentic Self. Once we have moved past this challenge, we become fully expressed, and extraordinarily comfortable in our unique personality.

There is no going back once we glimpsed higher Truth. It may feel uncomfortable at first, like a familiar limb is missing. Once conscious perception is part of our life, we continue to shift and change. We and it are no longer static or stagnant; we swim in its dynamic Nature. We either let it be or we feel stymied by our own resistance...because we have met a deeper meaning, a harmony in life that feels far more peaceful than anything we've known before.

There comes a point where we want liberation. We yearn for freedom from mind's regurgitations, which no longer match our newfound transcendence of negative thought-forms. Our commitment to release ourselves from life's dramas—to "cut it out" —causes us to focus on making good use of our mental energy, resulting in higher emotional energy frequencies. We reach for our full spiritual power. With consistent Presence, we eventually succeed and consciously allow higher inspiration to govern our thought processes. When truly readied to make our way (in a genuinely big way!) we are no longer run by the inner voices of the past.

When 'not in our control' transformative shifts are taking place, we are gentle with ourselves. We watch our fallibility with tenderness as we revisit stages, re-cycling our inner learning and being led by greater insight. Furthermore, we remember to decline the slippery slope of self-diminishment. Our intentional attention to "snap out of it," to realign our Beingness with the Eternal serves us well, as a reliable spiritual tool. Many choose deepened self-introspection and inquiry-based journaling for clearing stagnation or blocks. Some of us may be prone to states of mystical depression. Breath work, conscious devotional practices and revisits with spiritual study can assist us through these passages.

The ego-mind's favorite games include co-opting Spirit's leadership. In striking contrast to our new inner climate, reactive fear-energy's stepchildren—doubt, worry and control—signify that ego-mind is up to mischief (usually because we are up to being our Intrinsic Greatness). Resistant responses to life are *signals* that alert us to energy disconnect. Our earnest attention plays an integral role in returning us to peaceful centeredness, trusting that each step we take is one with a Univeral evolutionary process.

Once we know we are of Source energy, our consistent alignment with the truth of *what we came from, who we are, and who we will forever be* allows us to live with grace and ease. We have accepted that *we are cause* in the matters of our lives, health, wealth and joyfulness. Wholeness, a profound sense of Well-Being, is our very aliveness. We know it is our natural state. In recognition of the fact that we are Source energy's players in a field of consciousness, we also realize we can be blockages to its energy as well. As such we recognize any critical breakdown in life as a strong message from Source. Wake up calls arrive through our outer circumstances, including bodily malfunctions. The quality of our life reflects our vacillation of allowance and openness of Seventh Stage energy.

As we integrate the wisdom of this Seventh Life Process, we connect with our Higher Self throughout the day, nurturing our assuredness of Oneness with All-That-Is. Our personality blends into Who We Are without a need for worldly identity to justify our existence. We breathe each breath from a space of awareness of our divine union with Source. We have released attachment to a need for acknowledgment of our intrinsic greatness. Our experience validates our knowing that It rests within. We become adept at beginning each day anew, honoring our divine origins and alignment with Source.

Now we listen to our inner world, trusting the daily unfolding of life. Stage Seven shifts spark our empowerment to live in the mystery while actively engaged from the ground of our expanded consciousness. It is the stage of spiritual maturation in which our outer presence fully joins our Inner Being. Being focused in the physical *while* aligned with our invisible nonphysical energy is our powerful life-force alignment. We live in the present moment, appreciating the meaningful purpose of each day.

Seventh chakra opening heightens our intuition to such a degree that we are capable of experiencing uncommon illumination. Our genuine wisdom chooses to allow life to unfold with loving detachment. We perceive each micro-movement made in respect to a particular aspiration as an element that within itself contains the Whole. We sense the fullness of a matured oak tree within our acorn vision, with no evidence or agreement of outcome in sight. The constant spiritual gardeners with trust as infinite and enduring as the mustard seed, we move metaphoric mountains in our life. We *let go, let God* moment to moment, easily trusting as we go forward, thriving in the abundant nature of Life. With every endeavor or aspiration, we trust implicitly in the perfection of Life's process, living in appreciative memory of the moment we answered the call to Oneness.

Our Evolving Energy

When old habitual thoughts occur and we continue our practice of witnessing from Inner Being's conscious awareness and spaciousness appears. We experience moments in time when we are certain that we are not the concept or belief that we witnessed float through our mind. We have slowed down the mechanism of runaway, reactive thought patterns. We have observed, from a detached-impersonal viewpoint: who we are not and recognize fully Who in fact We Are. We now realize that pure consciousness pure potentiality is watching and rewriting the story of our life. We are inspired to engage in altruistic thoughts, words and deeds. We become potential participants in selfless humanitarianism, and our intentional attention is further focused on benevolent "cause-effect" scenarios.

Enlightened awareness responds to Life as a cosmic force: Life is All-That-Is. Separation dissolves when crown chakra openness awakens our Oneness awareness. From a broadened understanding and awakened knowledge, we now perceive good-and-bad dualities as elements of the same cosmic force, as causative factors of a grand evolutionary process.

Grounded in the Universal truth of evolutionary change, we are visionary catalysts helping humanity evolve. We commit equally to the natural process of our personal as well as planetary transformation. Whatever is unfolding is ideally perceived as elemental to our and all others' conscious evolution. Experiences in our environment are received as practice to strengthen this higher understanding. Once we arrive fully at home with seeming opposites, we relax knowing all events in life originate from the Whole.

Those tapped into the Core creative process are inspired to engage in proactive shifts of planetary consciousness. In these shifts, we let go what no longer works, and collaborate to co-create what does. Capable of living in a humble state of Wholeness, we recognize this same state of being is available to all who choose it. Knowing ourselves and all others as spirit-mind-body energy beings, we recognize engaged compassion as our original Nature. Our spiritual code of honor deems we embrace the universal truth: I or they would have done better if we had known consciously how.

Reverence for all of Life is Seventh Stage mystical wisdom. We see ourselves, as well as all others, as Divine Light. We know that we are doing the best we can from our current level of conscious awareness. Living from the values we hold dear to our Heart, we partake in inclusiveness and respect interdependence of all living beings. We know that all of life is Source energy and our presence is the power of Love's Light. We are moved by the cosmos, not by ego-intellect, and our immortal Light shines on one and all, everywhere we go.

Self-realized, we walk out into the world with certainty that our Presence fulfills our higher purpose. Any seeming lack or limitation, or momentary "flinch," is breathed through with our Heart's clear mindedness. Our presence is a blessing to all we meet. The peace we resonate is palpable. Our smile speaks wordless, compassionate love for all Others.

When our dynamic Stage Seven energy is active, some of us respond with hypersensitivity to artificial light, sound, the computer's electromagnetic emanations or other environmental factors. We grow to consciously care for our well being, having learned that self-care is a top priority. Until this energy energetic challenge balances, we utilize our resilient ability to discern, choosing wisely where we go and what we do. Our reverence for Life encourages spiritual discernment. Our environmental choices and behaviors reflect respect of our evolving energy. Our heightened receptivity of grace and ease enhances our ability to walk into any environment, to be with all people and circumstances.

Our Higher Knowing is our resonance meter. We remember to readily feel its signals when they alert us. We're most likely listening to our body's subtle energy signals and their relative chakra centers. Able to self-interpret what is at the heart of a matter, we breathe into it, allowing whatever arises to be held with our curiosity and trust.

Our connection with Source relieves a worldly need to prove ourselves. We realize there is nothing to prove as we are open and spacious divine beings. Ego-driven goals, the need to win at all costs, the impulse to control situations, and the misuse of personal power dissipate as conscious aspirations awakened in earlier stages focus our attentiveness.

Defensiveness and feelings of guilt disappear as we recognize there is nothing to defend or feel guilty about. We see our guiltlessness through eyes of the Universe, having reclaimed our Original innocence. Old psychological walls—defense, blame, guilt and shame—melt way. Surrendering our *I-me-mine* point of view, we experience life free of separating delusions.

Our connectivity with Infinite Intelligence boosts our intellect's organizing abilities. We capably recognize unifying patterns and see Divine order in Source-inspired intuitions. Our selection of passing pleasures in life is experienced and enjoyed with full awareness of the temporal nature of all things. We are less excitable and less prone to be set off balance by outer occurrences or inner dissonance, anchored by our commitment to being present.

Having accepted our sacred invitation to play in a stream of seamless moments called Life, we allow the Power that creates worlds to orchestrate the details of our human lives. While we cooperatively participate, we dance to our individual Soul's unique tune. As infinite immortal Being we trust the flow of life, curious of the future, freed from the past.

Life is *now*.

Seventh Self-Inquiry

Here we are. Another moment in time for slowing down with B R E A T H...

Enjoy some moments before you settle in and begin.

~ What is my understanding of God, Source-All That-Is? Describe in relation to your resonant highest knowing:

~ How often do I notice myself in past or future thinking inner dialogue? What is my most effective re-presencing tool?

~ Have I made a conscious commitment to connect with Source each day? What are my best practices? What works well to remain in ongoing alignment? What would I like to see shift in how I be with my practices?

~ If anything, what would I like to expand about my spiritual perspective? How might this empower my embodiment of Source energy flow?

~ How balanced and open am I to incoming shifts in conscious awareness? Describe your ideal state of openness:

~ What lingering habits of thought (beliefs) disrupt my ability to remain present: Elaborate on *how you be with* what you notice.

~ What is the content of my prayer requests? How often am I asking for 'things' to be different? How often do I focus on appreciation for what is?

~ How might I benefit by contemplation of the qualities of grace and ease? And by releasing patterns of resistance: for instance, doubt fear worry?

~ How do I respond when my inner questions do not manifest answers or insights in the way I desired? When no resolution appears for me to walk forward with?

~ What are my daily surrendering—*yield to what is*—practices? How do they enhance my moment-to-moment experience of Life?

~ What tests my trust in the Sacred process of transformative change? What is my current knowing and allowance of the expression "All Is Well"?

Micro Moves

Enjoy a moment of silent stillness.

Inhaling deeply and Exhaling fully....slowing down

**B r e a t h e... B r e a t h e... B r e a t h e...
for a nice pause in time....**

Okay to go?

Okay, here you go...

Ask yourself: *Where am I feeling stagnant or stuck?* Take some time with this...
b r e a t h e....into it...write a few answers down...

Pause a moment – Ready yourself to examine, discover and create new solutions –

Then:

What issue matters most to me—right here, right now?

What would I most like to change about this? What is it that I want to create instead?

Is this something I can do independent of support or professional guidance?

Would it be more self-loving to ask for help? If so, who will I enroll to support me?

And then:

What teeny action step would head me in the direction I desire?

★Notice what bubbles up…jot down as many as you like★

<u>Ask yourself</u>:

Which one specifically? What thrilled me, even felt a little scary?

When am I going to take this little step? Create a specific "by when" date + time of day.

Whom may I safely tell what I promised myself to do?

Who would respect me by simply listening?

And allow me to tell them I took this step?

*If you have a tried and true accountability structure, great! If not, having one is excellent support for the process of change.

*Enroll a mentor or trusted confidant. Create what works, maybe a "no reply requested" e-mail share.

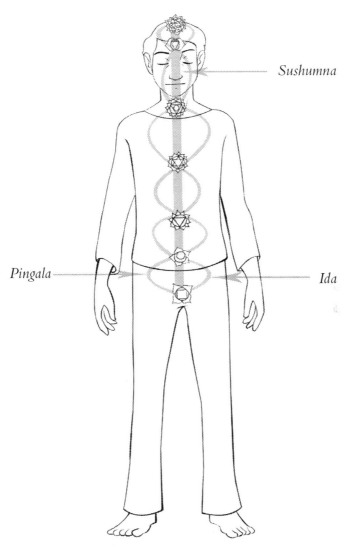

Sushumna

Pingala

Ida

"There are actually more than seven chakras, but seven main ones. Energy moves through channels or "nadis", the three main ones travel up the spine. They are called the ida, pingala and sushumna. The sushumna is the central channel through which— when balanced and open—the kundalini energy rises. The chakras are wheels of energy which we strive to balance."

Yoga Teacher Trainer—Tanya Greve, ERYT 500

RESOURCES

www.abrahamhicks.com

Caroline Joy Adams: www.carolinejoyadams.com, caroline@carolinejoyadams.com

The Coaches Training Institute (CTI): www.thecoaches.com/

Michael and Nina Prukop: www.ourintuitiveself.com, ourintuitiveself@yahoo.com

Peggy Daugherty ND CMT:www.manual-medicine.com (Manual Therapy for the treatment of chronic pain, stress and injuries., Specialist in Cranial Therapy. Offering private therapy sessions and advanced trainings)

Donna Iona Drozda: http://www.donnaionadrozda.com/

Rabia Erduman: www.wuweiwu.com/ (Alchemical Hypnotherapist and Registered Polarity Practioner)

Richard Carson and Associates: www.tamingyourgremlin.com

www.shiftnetwork.com

www.spiritualcimena circle.com

BIBLIOGRAPHY/RECOMMENDED READING

Andrews, Ted
Animal Speak: The Spiritual and Magical Powers of Creatures Great and Small
Llewellyn Publications, 2000

Bradshaw, John
Homecoming: *Reclaiming and Championing Your Inner Child*
Bantam, 1992

Carson, Rick
A Master Class in Gremlin-Taming: The Absolutely Indispensable Next Step for Freeing Yourself from the Monster of the Mind
HarperCollins, 2008

Carson, Rick
Taming Your Gremlin: A Surprisingly Simple Method for Getting Out of Your Own Way
HarperCollins, 2003

Chopra, Deepak
How to Know God: *The Soul's Journey Into the Mystery of Mysteries*
Harmony Books, 2000

Coehlo, Paulo
The Alchemist: *A Fable About Following Your Dream*
HarperSanFranscisco, 1995

Coehlo, Paulo
Aleph
Alfred A Knopf, 2011

A Course in Miracles
The Foundation for Inner Peace, 1975
Crane, George
Bones of the Master: *A Journey into Secret Mongolia*
Bantam Press, 2000

Deida, David
Dear Lover: *A Woman's Guide to Men, Sex and Love's Deepest Bliss*
Plexus, 2002

Erduman, Rabia
Veils of Separation: *Finding the Face of Oneness*
Self-published, 2001

Gach, Michael Reed
Acu-Yoga: *The Acupressure Stress Management Book*
Japanese Publications, 1981

Gawain, Shakti
Creative Visualization
Bantam Books, 1982

Golas, Thaddeus
The Lazy Man's Guide to Enlightenment
Author Self-published, 1972; Bantam Books, 1980

Goldberg, Natalie
Writing Down the Bones: *Freeing the Writer Within*
Shambhala Publications, 1986

Harvey, Bill
Mind Magic
Irvington Publishers, 1980

Hay, Louise L.
You Can Heal Your Life
Hay House, 1984

Hicks, Esther and Jerry (The Teachings of Abraham)
The Amazing Power of Deliberate Intent: *Living the Art of Allowing*
Hay House, 2006

Howard, Vernon
Mystic Path to Cosmic Power
Parket Publishing Company, 1967

Huxley, Aldous
Island: *A Novel*
Harper & Row, 1962

Jampolsky, M.D., Gerald G.
Good Bye to Guilt: *Releasing Fear Through Forgiveness*
Bantam Books, 1985

Jampolsky, M.D., Gerald G.
Love Is Letting Go of Fear
Celestial Arts, 1979

Judith, Anodea
Eastern Body Western Mind: *Psychology and the Chakra System as a Path to the Self*
Celestial Arts, 1996

Kabat-Zinn, Ph.D., John
Full Catastrophe Living: *Using the Wisdom of Your Body and Mind to Face Stress, Pain and Illness*
Bantam Dell, 1990

Katie, Byron, with Stephen Mitchell
Loving What Is: *Four Questions That Can Change your Life*
Three Rivers Press, 2002

Krishnamurti
Freedom From The Known
Harper Collins, 1969

May, M.D., Gerald G.
Addiction and Grace: *Love and Spirituality in the Healing of Addictions*
HarperSanFrancisco, 1988

Merton, Thomas
The Way of Chuang Tzu
New Directions, 1965

Myss, Ph.D. Caroline
Anatomy of the Spirit: *The Seven Stages of Power and Healing*
Three Rivers Press, 1996

Osho
Courage: *The Joy of Living Dangerously*
St. Martin's Griffin, 1999

Osho
Intuition: *Knowing Beyond Logic*
St. Martin's Griffin, 2001

Peers, E Allison
Dark Night of the Soul
Image, 1959

Pinkola Estes PhD., Clarrisa
Women Who Run With the Wolves: *Myths and Stories of the Wild Woman Archetype*
Ballantine Books, 1992

Roberts, Jane
The Nature of Personal Reality: *Specific, Practical Techniques for Solving Everyday Problems and Enriching the Life You Know.*
New World Library, 1974

Roberts, Jane
The Oversoul Seven Trilogy
Amber Allen, 1995

Ruiz, Don Miguel
The Four Agreements: *A Practical Guide to Personal Freedom*
Amber Allen Publishing, 1997

Ruiz, Don Miguel
The Mastery of Love: *A Practical Guide to the Art of Relationship*
Amber-Allen Publishing 1999

Sark
The Bodacious Book of Succulence: *Daring to Live your Succulent Wild Life!*
Fireside, 1998

Small, Jacquelyn
Awakening Time: *The Journey from Codependence to Co-Creation*
Bantam Books, 1991

Starr, Mirabai
Night of the Soul: *St. John of the Cross Dark*
New Translation and Introduction by Mirabai Starr
Riverhead Books, 2002

Tolle, Eckhart
A New Earth: *Awakening to Your Life's Purpose*
A Plume Book, 2005

Tolle, Eckhart
The Power of Now: *A Guide to Spiritual Enlightenment*
New World Library, 1999

Weston, M.D., Trevor
Know Your Body: *The Atlas of Anatomy*
Ulysses Press, 1985-95

Wilde, Stuart
Infinite Self: *33 Steps to Reclaiming Your Inner Power*
Hay House, 1996

Zukav, Gary
The Seat of the Soul
A Fireside Book, Simon & Schuster, 1989

Zweig, Connie, and Jeremiah Abrams, ed.
Meeting the Shadow: *The Hidden Power of the Dark Side of Human Nature*
Jeremy P. Tarcher, Inc., 1991

ABOUT THE AUTHOR

Antoinette Levine is an author, wisdom walker-way shower, nature lover and yoga practitioner living vibrantly in Ojai, CA. Antoinette began her lifelong study of Eastern spiritual traditions, spiritual metaphysics and consciousness-raising studies at 18 years of age. Majoring in psychology while attending the University of California at Santa Barbara, she began Para-professional counseling which  eventually would lead to Life Coaching/Spiritual Guidance work. After transferring to the University of Southern California she earned her Bachelor of Arts Degree in Journalism and Public Relations. Her thirty-six year career in the media and Motion Picture industries catalyzed Ms. Levine's inspirational leadership, which included mentoring up and coming creative professionals.

For more info: www.AntoinetteLevine.com

Printed in the United States
By Bookmasters